PRACTICAL TASKS

Terry Russell started his career in education as a primary school teacher before working as an educational psychologist. His interest in children's cognitive development has been located particularly in the area of science concepts. He worked with the Assessment of Performance Unit (APU) primary science assessment team before moving to Liverpool to become Director of the Centre for Research in Primary Science and Technology.

Wynne Harlen, after graduating in physics at Oxford, taught in schools and colleges for a number of years before moving into research and curriculum development in primary science. She was engaged in the evaluation of, first the Oxford Primary Science project and then Science 5/13, at Bristol University from 1966 to 1973, gaining a PhD through research into evaluation procedures. For the next four years at Reading University, she led the Progress in Learning Science project which produced the 'Match and Mismatch' materials. During this time she edited *Evaluation and the Teacher's Role* for the Schools Council and contributed to a number of other publications on curriculum evaluation, including *Values and Evaluation* and *Evaluation Roles*. She moved to London University in 1977 to what is now King's College, where she was deputy director of the APU science project, until her appointment in January 1985 as Sidney Jones Professor of Science Education in the University of Liverpool.

Assessing Science in the Primary
Classroom

PRACTICAL TASKS

TERRY RUSSELL and WYNNE HARLEN

P·C·P
Paul Chapman
Publishing Ltd

Copyright © 1990 Terry Russell and Wynne Harlen

Paul Chapman Publishing Ltd
144 Liverpool Road
London
N1 1LA

British Library Cataloguing in Publication Data
Russell, Terry 1946–
    Practical tasks.
    1. Great Britain. Primary schools. Curriculum subjects:
    Science. Academic achievement of students. Assessment
    I. Title   II. Harlen, Wynne   III. Series
    372.35

    ISBN 1-85396-078-0

Typeset by DP Photosetting, Aylesbury, Bucks
Printed by St Edmundsbury Press, Bury St Edmunds, England
Bound by W.H. Ware, Clevedon, Avon

A B C D E F 5 4 3 2 1 0

Contents

General introduction to the STAR series

During the past decade, increasing attention has been paid to the provision of science in the primary school. The desire to improve the quality of this provision has been a feature not only of the educational debate in the United Kingdom but also in other industrialized countries. It is, for example, the major focus of the Council of Europe's current educational programme. This attention stems largely from the realization that today's primary children need to be more 'scientifically literate' than previous generations were, if they are to solve the problems which will face them when they enter the world of work in the 21st century. The provision of Educational Support Grants (ESG) to local authorities and the elevation of science as a core curriculum area in the National Curriculum both illustrate the Government's determination to improve the quality of science teaching in our schools.

Earlier attempts to improve the provision of science in the primary school gave rise to large-scale projects funded by the then Schools Council. This approach was too simplistic, particularly in the assumption made about the willingness of teachers to commit themselves to changes which they themselves did not help to create. More recently school-focused curriculum research has tried to remedy this deficiency. However, the pragmatic approach generally adopted has made it difficult to transfer the practice developed within one school to others who did not participate in the original development.

The Science Teacher Action Research (STAR) project has tried to combine the advantages of 'project based' and 'school-focused curriculum development' approaches. While the STAR team provided a conceptual framework for teaching science at primary level, the application of this framework, in the form of tasks which were appropriate for children of different abilities and ages, was left to the teachers who participated in the project. It was hoped that the teaching of primary science in this way, while informed by theory would also be practical. A key element in this strategy was to provide participating teachers with appropriate means of assessing pupil performance in different aspects of the scientific processes. While the close association between what is taught and what is assessed has long been recognized, it is only recently that the positive aspects of this relationship have been appreciated. Assessment procedures which reflect the objectives of the curriculum, not only tend to ensure closer correspondence between the intentions of those who develop the curriculum and the observed practice of those who implement it but also provide a common language, based on shared understandings of the learning processes involved. Such 'shared understandings' were essential in the STAR project if the participating teachers were to play a full part in its development.

As is now generally recognized, no one method of assessment enjoys sufficient advantages over others to ensure its exclusive use. Reliable judgements of pupil performance need to take into account the capacity of children to achieve in a variety of contexts. In the STAR project, attention was given to the performance of pupils on written tasks, during practical activities and in the context of general classroom work where teachers carried out systematic observation as part of their general monitoring procedure. Each of these approaches yields information which can be entered into a profile of pupil achievement, combining the advantages and minimizing the disadvantages of each respective method.

The STAR project was based jointly at the Department of Education of Liverpool University and the School of Education of Leicester University, from 1986 to the end of 1989. This is one of three books emerging from the project's work. It is concerned with the assessment of practical activity in science through a combination of observation of a child's actions and discussions with the child to reveal the thinking associated with these actions. It describes the procedures and results of using a specially designed activity, the Water Sprinkler task, for the assessment of children's science process skills in the project. This account is placed in the context of a wider discussion of practical assessment which can be applied in regular classroom activities and in other areas of the curriculum than science. We hope, therefore, that the book will serve a useful purpose for all who work in primary science.

Maurice Galton and Wynne Harlen
Series Editors

Acknowledgments

We should like to acknowledge the involvement of Cheshire, Leicester, Sheffield and Wirral Education Authorities and the co-operation and encouragement given by the following local authority education advisers:

Brian Leek	(Cheshire)
Roy Illsley	(Leicestershire)
Roy Jefferson	(Sheffield)
Charles Harrison	(Wirral)

who also constituted a Consultative Committee to advise the project team. We are indebted to each authority for making available their advisory teacher teams, and would like to acknowledge the commitment and work of:

Keith Roberts (1986–7)	
Roger Walker (1986–7)	(Cheshire)
Gerry Phillips (1986–7)	
Annette Drake (1987–9)	
Sue Eland	(Leicestershire)
Geoff Tite	
Linda Gatens	(Sheffield)
Di Sutton	(Wirral)
Elaine Weatherhead	

In particular, we should wish to recognize the contributions made by Gareth Williams (who was seconded to the project for the Autumn term of 1986, by Wirral LEA and who contributed significantly to the development of the practical assessment task described in this book), and by the teachers in whose classes so much of the work was carried out:

Chris Abbott   Tricia Adams   Jane Armstrong   Anne Baird   Suzanne Beard
Bobbie Blakemore   Lynn Brayley   Lesley Broady   Carol Brown   Linda Burton
Fred Chadwick   Christine Cowlard   Karen Creedon   Steve Dakin   Mike
Delaney   Alastair Dodd   Jan Eastwood   Jane Elders   Louise Ellis   Robert
Elverstone   Anne Ezard   Peter Faragher   Christine Fisher   Lorraine Garnham
Mark Genower   Barbara Greenwood   Tim Griffiths   David Harker   Eileen
Harrigan   Roger Harrison   Jeremy Harwood   Diane Hawkins   Eddie Hunt
Maraide Hurst   Chris Hyland   Joyce Jackson   Judy Jackson   Stuart Jameson
Eirian Jones   Dawn King   Nigel Kingdon   Dave Leavesley   Frank Lewis   Sue
Lyonette   Jan McDonald   Paul Maddox   Sue Manford   Meg Marshall   Martin
Midgley   Pam Moody   Graham Morton   Geraldine Murphy   Margaret Noble
Conrad North   Janet Pilling   Jan Ratherham   Steve Reeds   Jane Sheard
Maureen Skelton   Barbara Staniland   Mari Street   Dawn Strover   Paul Stubbs
Delphine Sullivan   Gerry Till   Felicity Titley   Margaret Turner   Anne Vickers
Caroline Wardle   Gwen Williams   Mark Williams   Roger Woolnough.

Terry Russell and
Wynne Harlen,
1990.

Introduction

The elevation of science to the status of a core subject within the National Curriculum was a radical, though generally welcomed, step. It had the greatest implications at the primary level where, although considerable progress had been made in the 1980s, the extent of good practice and confidence in teaching science was still limited. The combination in the National Curriculum for science of attention to the processes and methods of science (in Attainment Target (AT) 1: The Exploration of Science) and the requirement for assessment to become part of teaching, has put the assessment of process skills into the forefront of attention.

Science is about understanding certain aspects of the physical world around us and it involves testing and changing ideas about how natural and made things work. Practical investigation is central to scientific activity of all kinds, whether carried out by scientists or by children at school. Certainly, some practising scientists are theoreticians, but the ultimate test of their ideas is whether or not they work in practice: they use their theories to make predictions and then see to what extent these fit the real world. The activity of children learning science is similar. They also begin from their ideas about how things are and change and develop these ideas by testing them out in practical investigations. This similarity is pointed out in the National Curriculum Non-Statutory Guidance (NCC, 1989), extending the argument to highlight the role of process skills:

> For the child learning science, as for the scientist, the way understanding develops depends both on existing ideas and on the processes by which those ideas are used and tested in new situations.

The experience of children is limited, and thus their ideas may well not be consistent with scientific ones, which are based on a far greater range of evidence. However, if a child's ideas are consistent with the evidence which is available to him or her, then they are as scientific as those of scientists even though much less widely applicable.

Young children's limited experience also means that they are restricted in abstract and theoretical thinking: things have to be encountered in reality before they can be the subject of thought and mental manipulation. Thus the provision of this experience of objects and events around them is essential to their mental development. This is another way of saying that first-hand investigation is central to learning science for young children. Its value is not only in terms of giving information through the senses about the world, but also the realisation that investigation can provide answers and that they themselves can learn from their own interaction with things around them.

It is not possible to distinguish practical activity from mental activity, and so we are concerned with far more than the physical manipulation of objects and the ability to use equipment effectively. Practical activity must involve planning based on hypothesising and prediction, the gathering of information by observation and, perhaps, by measurement; the control of variables; interpretation of data; and the recording and communication of results. In each of these, there is a combination of mental and physical activity.

Before the advent of the APU (Assessment of Performance Unit), it was widely assumed that the processes involved in practical science were not susceptible to reliable assessment. The APU work demonstrated that this was not the case by developing and using a wide range of both written and practical tests of process skills such as observation, interpretation, planning, communicating, and hypothesising (see Russell *et al.*, 1988). This work also revealed some of the difficulties and issues relating to assessment of processes. In particular, it was realised that while some process skills can be assessed separately and, sometimes, quite adequately on paper (e.g. interpretation and planning), this information does not say anything about how well children can carry out scientific investigations in practice.

The assessment of practical investigations is the focus of this book. The ideas in it arose from the work of the Science Teaching Action Research (STAR) project, which began long before the National Curriculum came on the scene. STAR was a programme of action research into the teaching and learning of primary science, and was in operation from January 1986 until late 1989. Its particular focus was to help teachers change practices so that pupils had more opportunity to use and develop process skills. Part of the work involved producing methods of observing and assessing children's performance in process skills. In doing this, the project had, not surprisingly, to meet and tackle many of the difficulties in defining and assessing development in practical skills which are now being faced more widely.

For those teachers and advisers who have supported science activities in primary schools for many years, this book may be useful in that it scrutinises the fine detail of AT1: Exploration of Science and the implications for assessment in this area. For others there may be much that feels unfamiliar in teaching and assessing science, and before they make radical changes to their practice, some sort of map of the terrain might be appreciated. For such teachers, this book offers two main sources of support. First, there is a detailed description of what exploration of science entails, what its component parts are, and how the practical process skills of science are described within the terms of the National Curriculum. Second, the book gives a wealth of examples of the kinds of things that children do and say when engaged in scientific investigations. Putting these two aspects together – the practical process criteria on the one hand and children's responses on the other – we have the opportunity to consider issues of how to assess performance against criteria. This makes it possible to describe and exemplify criterion-referenced assessment in a way that should be both immediate and comprehensible.

Now familiar or unfamiliar are the science process skills? In many teachers' experience, primary science has its roots in nature study and environmental studies. These are both disciplines with a sound primary pedigree: the former tended to be based on young children's apparent predisposition to be fascinated with the natural world; the latter tends to be cross-curricular and, most important, adds an exploratory dimension. Many of the apprehensions about the formal introduction of science into primary classrooms might stem from a misapprehension that it will be an import of an entire subject discipline from secondary schools. This is not at all the case. Good practice in primary science exploits children's natural interests and curiosity. It is mostly investigatory in character, but it also requires children to take on some of the discipline and rigour of scientific enquiries.

Primary science is not just a matter of **knowing about** the world; there is an equally emphatic goal of helping children to **behave as scientists** in the world. While both aspects are important and relevant to science in the primary school, the distinction between **conceptual** understanding and **procedural** knowledge is a fundamental and useful one. Conceptual understanding is concerned with the ideas of science: concepts such as what is a plant and what distinguishes plants from animals; what is sound, how it is generated, how it travels, how the human ear receives sound energy; what the characteristics of different materials are and how they behave under different conditions. Scientific concepts are more than just isolated 'facts', in the sense that they may be ideas about quite complex relationships between things. The distinction between plant and animal, for example, is a complex matter which must be described by reference to the structures and processes of each (with some marginal and unexplained cases such as fungi and viruses left over).

Science processes describe the ways of behaving scientifically. We might describe most of our daily behaviour as 'common-sensical', though it takes place in the same world and with many of the same objects and phenomena which may, in other circumstances, be the subject of interest or enquiry within a science activity. For example, we cross the road and make judgements about the velocity of vehicles which we must avoid. Such decisions are not made 'scientifically' – it would be a waste of time and effort and very few roads would ever be crossed. Instead, for safety reasons, we simply allow generous margins in our judgements. Everyday judgements are made for 'here-and-now'. Scientific judgements attempt to embody greater generality. They also aspire to convince others of their truth and application and to do this must be based on certain procedural rules. These rules are not simply arbitrary or legalistic; they have their own consistency, logic and progression, providing a framework within which deductions can be drawn. Applying them provides what is sometimes referred to as 'scientific rigour'; an attempt to be more objective, for example by using measurement, usually implies that the investigation or experiment can be replicated by someone else, to challenge or confirm a reported finding.

Those who might be tempted to claim that children's explorations within broad cross-curricular topics or environmental studies is necessarily science under a different name, must be able to show that the children's work has the specific discipline of scientific investigation. The regret of the advocates of primary science has often been that the potential science component becomes diluted or runs out between the cracks in cross-curricular topics. This book is concerned with the science-specific process skills: not observation as it happens in language work, but observation as it is approached in science, to cite just one example. Such skills need not be thought of as being acquired all at once. It is possible to map out some sort of progression such that even the youngest children can start out on the route of behaving 'scientifically'.

A brief history of the origins of the STAR project, its roots and its aspirations might prove reassuring, for it anticipated many of the issues with which the implementation of the National Curriculum confronts teachers. The background to and aims of the Primary STAR Project are described in Chapter 1. Assessment was fundamental to the project, because it was concerned to examine and describe in detail the kinds of science activities that could be identified, which might be promoted within classrooms. The varieties of practical assessment and the advantages and disadvantages of each are described in detail in the next chapter, together with a consideration of the **purposes** of assessment – the arguments for which were well rehearsed in the report of the Task Group on Assessment and Testing (DES, 1988).

The issue of the **progression** of skills is another key idea within the National Curriculum, and Chapter 2 emphasizes the developmental aspect of process skills. Assessment must take this developmental aspect seriously. If it is to be effective for formative purposes, teachers will need to use assessment as the basis for formulating the next learning experience. Furthermore, if progression is to be assessed, general descriptions will not be sufficient; progressive development within the process skills will need to be described in very specific terms. This is precisely what the STAR practical assessment criteria attempted to do, and comparisons with the National Curriculum criteria provide an interesting comparison. Together, Chapters 1 and 2 present and discuss the theoretical considerations underpinning practical assessment criteria used by STAR and represented within the National Curriculum.

Chapters 3, 4 and 5 present an example of a practical task and discuss its development, administration and scoring. The practical assessment activities are centred on the phenomenon of a plastic bottle, suspended by a thread, set spinning by jets of water escaping from holes in its base. The actual content is not of over-riding importance as many other starting points would have served equally well. The discussion is concerned with the ways in which children thought and acted in relation to the task that was presented. The skills that are described and discussed are of a general nature, but are best exemplified in some concrete form. The task **could** be replicated with children as a way for teachers to gain direct experience of the skills that are described; equally, variants on the same repertoire of skills should be seen in any practical science investigation in any classroom in which opportunities for exploration of science are provided.

The final section of the book, Chapter 6, takes all the issues raised in earlier chapters into the context of classroom implementation. It is clear that assessment will be a major consideration of every teacher within the terms of the National Curriculum. Assessment and testing seems to mean different things to different people; for some, the administrative burden is the pre-eminent implication. Whatever the external demands, teachers will always have a need to monitor the progress of children within their classes. A new core subject raises its own particular problems and demands. In this chapter, every effort is made to offer support to teachers with integrating assessment of practical science activities into their everyday practice, so that it becomes a manageable and useful activity.

1

A Framework for Practical Assessment

Practical assessment in science takes a wide variety of forms. Almost the only common feature across this range is that items of equipment or objects of some sort are used by those being assessed. Features in which practical assessment methods differ include whether or not:

- the actions carried out are observed and recorded on the spot;
- an end product is left behind and assessed after the event;
- a written record of the activity and findings is the basis of assessment;
- there is some interaction between the person assessing and the one being assessed in which questions are put and answers noted.

In addition, situations can vary according to whether the task is an individual or a group one, whether or not there is a time limit and whether or not the situation is perceived as a test or as special in some way, or just as normal work.

Examples of these varieties are more familiar from secondary schooling, and occur in other subjects as well as science. Instrumental music examinations are instances where on the spot performance is assessed with some limited and highly structured interaction of examiner with student. In a foreign language oral test, the interaction takes a more central role and again there is no end product. A practical science examination uses a combination of observation and written record as evidence of performance.

A further variation relates to the design of the task, which can be narrowly focused on a specific, practical skill or process skill, or designed to require the orchestration of a number of skills. This dimension is an important one in science, although no doubt it has its parallel in other 'practical' assessment. For instance, it is seen in the distinction between assessing ability to play scales or arpeggios in a musical examination, and assessing the performance of a study in which the agility of scale playing has to be combined with many other techniques and with artistic expression. It is the distinction between pronouncing words correctly in a foreign language and being able to sustain a meaningful conversation in the language.

Some examples of sharply-focused and more broadly-designed practical tasks in science help to convey the meaning of this distinction and to highlight the pros and cons of each against the other. Both kinds were used in the APU science surveys (Russell *et al.*, 1988) which provide the following examples.

In the fourth APU survey of 11 year olds, performance in 'Observation' was assessed by a series of short items presented in a practical 'circus' (a set of activities which are visited and performed by each child in turn in varying sequence). In one such item, children were presented with seven types of small seed (some being spices) (Figure 1.1):

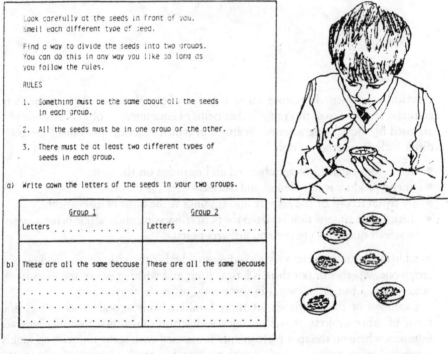

Look carefully at the seeds in front of you.
Smell each different type of seed.

Find a way to divide the seeds into two groups.
You can do this in any way you like so long as
you follow the rules.

RULES

1. Something must be the same about all the seeds
    in each group.

2. All the seeds must be in one group or the other.

3. There must be at least two different types of
    seeds in each group.

a) Write down the letters of the seeds in your two groups.

Group 1	Group 2
Letters	Letters . . . .
b) These are all the same because	These are all the same because
. . . .	. . . .
. . . .	. . . .
. . . .	. . . .
. . . .	. . . .

Figure 1.1   *APU observation task: 'seeds'.*

In another there was a sealed matchbox with two small objects inside (Figure 1.2).

These items can be seen to require the use of the senses (touch, smell, hearing and sight) followed by some interpretation of the information obtained. They could be completed quite quickly, so that a number of items with different subject matter could be used. This is an important consideration when the skills are the focus of the assessment, since the APU results themselves show that the subject matter and context influence performance appreciably, and so the greater the variety of contexts represented, the less the bias caused by the particular ones used. We shall return to this point again in later discussion.

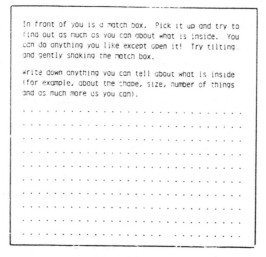

In front of you is a match box. Pick it up and try to
find out as much as you can about what is inside. You
can do anything you like except open it! Try tilting
and gently shaking the match box.

Write down anything you can tell about what is inside
(for example, about the shape, size, number of things
and as much more as you can).

Figure 1.2 *APU observation task: 'matchbox'.*

Another example of assessment of a discrete skill was the use of selected measuring instruments in the 1984 survey during individual practical tests. For example, the correct use of a thermometer was tested by giving a child a beaker of warm water poured from a flask and asking the child to find out how hot the water was using a thermometer. The reading was checked on the spot by the tester who was present throughout and could observe how the thermometer was used – whether the child removed it from the water to read it, as if it were a clinical thermometer, for instance.

In addition, the APU surveys of 11 year olds also included a small number of extended investigations, where children were given a broadly expressed problem, a range of equipment which was more than was required, and allowed (within a reasonable limit) to spend as much time as they needed in tackling the problem. One such investigation is shown in Figure 1.3.

The equipment included a large, shallow tray, live mealworms and four different kinds of food. A tester was present throughout and noted actions on a check-list. At the end of the investigation, the tester asked questions to probe reasons for certain actions and to elicit information that could not be gathered merely by observation.

These APU examples represent alternative approaches to the assessment of process skills through tasks focusing either on specific skills or on 'whole' investigations. Neither is without its advantages and disadvantages, which is important to consider because of the relevance to assessing Attainment Target 1 of the National Curriculum for science. In this, AT separate skills are identified in the Statements of Attainment, although the Programmes of Study indicate that these skills are to be developed in the context of explorations and investigations set within the context of children's everyday experience.

> Find out if the mealworms prefer to eat
> some of these foods more than others if
> they are given a choice.

a)   Use this space for notes about your tests and results
     as you go along :

b)   Put here what you found about the food the mealworms
     prefer :

     . . . .
     . . . .

Figure 1.3   *Investigation of mealworm food preference.*

The advantages of the discrete process skill tasks are:

- they can be designed to require only the intended skill and so the assessment of this skill is more 'pure', not depending on other abilities;
- they are short and so several tasks can be given to assess performance in the context of different subject matter;
- they direct children to perform particular tasks and so the children can always do something in response and so have a sense of achievement.

Their disadvantages are:

- they may seem artificial and lacking purpose, which may lead to reduced motivation to perform well;
- in order to ensure that the particular process skill is used, what is required has to be clearly signalled by instructions, and so performance does not indicate whether the child would choose to use the process skill in that situation if not directed to do so.

For the whole investigation approach, the points for and against are more or less the reverse of these. The advantages are:

- they present real problems and some time for pupils to become involved, and so better motivated to perform well;
- there is a greater validity since skills are normally used in combination rather than one at a time;
- the assessment indicates pupils' ability to use process skills in solving problems where they have to choose to use them.

The disadvantages are:

- performance of process skills required at a later part of the investigation may depend on what has been done earlier (e.g. if no relevant observations have been made then no interpretation of them can be made);

- they are necessarily time consuming and this, among other things, imposes a severe limit on the contexts which can be represented;
- their validity for particular children depends on whether the children have been used to tackling whole problems by investigation following a set of instructions.

In the APU questions, the first of these disadvantages was minimized by a series of specified 'prompts' from the tester so that a child could be assisted to try a later part of the investigation, whatever happened earlier.

The APU examples, while differing in their 'whole' or 'discrete' approach, are the same in the important respect that they are all test situations, specially structured and set up so that information can be gained about how children tackle specified tasks. As such they have the advantages that:

- they give the children the opportunity to show what they can do in situations specially designed to require the use of practical and process skills;
- they provide standard conditions that are required for certain purposes of assessment;
- not least, they give teachers exemplification of activities and ways of questioning children which encourage the use of skills.

At the same time they share the disadvantages of practical tests, which include the following:

- tests can usually be given only infrequently, and so cannot be used to give feedback about progress on a regular basis;
- they often require special arrangements and always take up time from teaching and learning;
- they cause anxiety in many children, and sometimes in their teachers and parents, too, which is transmitted to children and adds to the stress they feel;
- the situations or problems, however carefully devised to be 'real', nevertheless come 'out of the blue' to the children, who may not be able to 'get into' the problem as if it were one they had chosen to take up for themselves;
- the same situations or problems are given to all and so, given the previous point, this is more like equal unfairness than equal fairness;
- the time taken for practical tasks means that only a few can be used, and so differences in interest in the subject matter (particularly gender-related ones) may have a considerable influence; had the problem been about something different, then the result may well have been different too;
- if the administration is to individual children rather than to groups, this may have a backwash into the curriculum against the cooperative group work which is needed for practical activities and for much effective learning.

When an effort is made to overcome these disadvantages, it leads in the direction of assessing children in situations which are similar to 'normal' learning activities. Indeed, **if** normal activities give opportunity for children to use and develop the practical and process skills relating to investigation, then they also provide opportunity for these skills to be assessed. The 'if' indicates an important precondition, however. If it does not exist, then the opportunity for assessment has to be provided by introducing specially-devised situations.

These considerations reveal, therefore, another dimension of variation of practical assessment, of which the two extreme ends are:

test situations _____ normal work

Between these two it is possible to envisage something less formal than a test, but more structured than normal work: special activities that have been devised so that children are required to use practical and process skills and which thus provide opportunity for assessment. The 'Water Sprinkler' activity described in Chapter 3 and 4 is an example of such a 'special activity'. But before setting the context for the description of this activity, it is important to have in mind some points about the purposes for which assessment can be carried out, since features that are a disadvantage for one purpose may be less so for another.

PURPOSES AND METHODS OF ASSESSMENT

Among the points made about the advantages and disadvantages of test situations were several whose importance will vary according to the **purpose** of the assessment. For example, if the purpose is to summarize achievement at a particular time in a way which enables pupils to be grouped together or compared with each other, then some degree of uniformity in the task given to different pupils becomes an advantage. If, on the other hand, the purpose is essentially to inform day-to-day decisions about the appropriate work and help needed by individual pupils, then it is important to assess the child in a task which makes demands which are neither too great nor too small. This may mean providing different tasks for different pupils.

Although a number of separate purposes of assessment can be identified, it is perhaps most useful here to consider them as being of four main kinds, using terms brought into general usage by the report of the Task Group on Assessment and Testing (TGAT):

- *formative*, so that the positive achievements of pupils may be recognized and discussed and the appropriate next steps may be planned;
- *diagnostic*, through which learning difficulties may be scrutinized and classified so that appropriate remedial help and guidance can be provided;
- *summative*, for the recording of the overall achievement of a pupil in a systematic way;
- *evaluative*, by means of which some aspects of the work of a school, an LEA or other discrete part of the educational service can be assessed and/or reported upon.
      (DES, 1988, para 23)

For discussion, these purposes of assessment can be reduced to two: formative (which can include diagnostic) and summative. Formative purposes, as defined by TGAT, and diagnostic purposes, have much in common. They are concerned with finding out regularly about children's current achievement in order to identify their needs and ways of helping their progress. Both formative and diagnostic assessment require detailed information about a child's achievement in relation to all the skills, knowledge and attitudes that the school aims to develop. The information must also be as reliable as possible for each individual child, which means the child must be in a position to perform well – not feeling anxious or under pressure or under- or overstretched. In general, normal classroom work provides the ideal situation for formative assessment, given the conditions mentioned earlier, that this includes all the required learning opportunities.

Summative purposes serve the needs of those who require to know what a child can do at a particular time. These include parents who receive an oral and/or written report at the end of each term, the receiving teacher when children move from one class to another and the teacher who wants to review achievement over a period of time in order to plan the next area of work. The information required can be readily provided from the on-going formative assessment, by summarizing achievement at a particular point in time. This summary would be essentially descriptive and qualitative.

Summative assessment is, however, sometimes seen as more judgemental and quantitative. The information may be derived from a summative test – of which commercial achievement tests, reading tests and the GCSE are examples – or by condensing the information accumulated formatively. The TGAT report pointed out that the summative purposes of National Assessment could be served by aggregating information gained for formative purposes, but the mechanisms for doing this, proposed later, involve quantifying different kinds of performance, which make the ultimate summary meaningless in terms of what children can actually do. For example, applying the rule that three out of four statements of attainment indicate achievement of a level, makes the information of dubious value since it is not known which three statements, or indeed whether all four, apply. It is in this way that quantification loses useful information.

For the National Curriculum Assessment the methods used to carry out the formative assessment is continuous assessment by teachers (Teacher Assessment, TA). This assessment is intended to be part of everyday work, which, since it must cover the National Curriculum, should provide all the opportunities needed for achievement in relation to the Attainment Targets to be assessed. The TGAT report also recommended that Standard Assessment Tasks (SATs) be used in addition to TA in order to 'provide standardized, i.e. nationally comparable assessment results' (para. 345). It also saw these tasks as serving the important function of clarifying the meaning of the statements of attainment in the curriculum in terms of what has to be learned. Recognizing the shadow of an assessment-led curriculum in this proposal, TGAT said:

In the past what is to be assessed has often been the only clear expression of what is to be taught and this has often led to a narrowing of the curriculum. This tendency can be reduced if the process can start from agreement about what has to be learned in terms of attainment targets.

(DES 1988, para. 56)

Thus SATs may be regarded as an aid, both in implementing the curriculum and to teacher assessment. This echoes the suggestion made earlier that some 'special activities' may be necessary to foster the assessment of science process skills. Help through exemplifying the skills in action in the classroom is particularly needed in science since, in many classrooms, the teaching of the subject is as much an innovation as the systematic assessment of it. This brings us back to the 'Water Sprinkler' activity and the particular purposes for which it was devised and the wider function it may have in National Curriculum assessment.

THE STAR PROJECT

As mentioned earlier, STAR stands for Science Teaching Action Research, and was the title of a programme of action research into the teaching and learning of primary science which was based jointly at University of Liverpool and University of Leicester from the beginning of 1986 to the end of 1989. When the project was conceived, there was concern about the extent and quality of science in the primary schools following the poor report in the HMI survey (DES, 1978) and the subsequent publication of findings of the Assessment of Performance Unit (Harlen et al., 1981, 1983, 1984). The need to improve practice in primary science and to find ways of spreading good practice was underlined by the clear statement by the DES in *Science: A Statement of Policy* that 'science should have a place in the education of all pupils of compulsory school age' (DES, 1985). This intention was later translated into law when science was designated a 'core' subject in the National Curriculum.

However, the means of implementing this change in the status of science was not at all clear, since there was, until the late 1980s, a dearth of research into the teaching and learning of science at primary level. There was no lack of good classroom material available, and so the solution was not to be found in producing more teacher or pupil material; neither was the provision of equipment and non-book resources necessarily the answer since there was evidence that much of what was available in schools was under-used. The APU surveys showed an increasing incidence of **some** science being taught in **some** schools, but at the same time revealed information about the way in which it was taught which gave cause for concern. In particular a very narrow range of process skills were used by children:

schools are providing suitable opportunities for the children to develop general skills such as observing, measuring and keeping records . . . there is now need to consider how to help children to acquire those more specific science skills such as defining patterns in observations, giving explanations, predicting, hypothesizing, controlling variables and planning investigations, in which children are much less competent.

(Harlen et al., 1983).

The STAR project was designed to assist in meeting this need by focusing on ways of helping teachers to change their practices so as to provide for their children the experiences through which they might develop the full range of science process skills.

In order to achieve its aims, the project worked with and through teachers, taking their starting points as the place from which to begin. The concept of what was 'good practice' was worked out in the classroom context, taking into account the constraints upon teachers and the conditions which exist in real classrooms. If this is not done, and some theoretical ideal notion of what teachers and pupils should be doing is proposed, there is very little chance of much change in practice occurring. The approach through 'action research' meant that the project team helped teachers to make changes in their classrooms which teachers themselves identified as being required; subsequently, the team monitored and fed back information to the teachers so that they could judge the extent to which they were being successful in their endeavour. Using this approach was felt to be an important part of the message: if teachers were given ownership of the ideas used in improving learning opportunities in their classrooms, they would experience what it was intended they should try to facilitate for their children, that is, ownership of the scientific ideas they were developing and a feeling of being in control of their learning.

To explain the role played by practical testing a brief outline of the project is necessary.

The work in schools (about 50 were involved, from four LEAs) was organized in three phases, each extending over one school year. The first phase was one of gathering data about the teaching and learning in the schools before any 'action' took place. The information about classroom events was collected by systematic observation using a schedule devised to focus on the use of science process skills. Observations of children's activity were made and recorded in successive two-minute intervals throughout a lesson. This instrument, known as SPOC (Science Processes Observation Categories), was devised by the project team and is described in *Assessing Science in the Primary Classroom: Observing Activities* (Cavendish *et al.*, 1990). It was used several times during the year to record science sessions. Meanwhile, the performance of pupils in process skills was assessed in two ways: by written tasks, incorporated into the work of the children by the teacher; and by an extended practical activity, administered to individual children by a tester (a team member or an LEA advisory teacher released by the LEA to join the project team).

The data collected in phase one was presented to the teachers at a conference which marked the transition to phase two. Views about the role of process skills in learning science were exchanged at this conference, and the research results were used by teachers to decide the focus and goals of changes which they would attempt to make in phase two, bearing in mind what was possible in their own schools and classrooms. Meetings of teachers, with input from the team and from each other, provided ideas of how, for example, more opportunties might be given for children to extend their observation, or to have experience of planning investigations, or raise questions of the kind to which they could find answers through interaction and practical enquiry. Classes were again observed while teachers were attempting to implement the changes they had planned, but in this phase, the observers provided immediate feedback after the lesson and discussed the implications for further action. Children were also assessed (in most cases a sample only of pupils in each class, selected to cover the ability range and both boys and girls) using the written tasks. Teachers were involved in marking their children's responses so that they had direct access to how their children were performing. This was often a key factor in the choice of focus for action – having rather more impact than the overall statistics produced about how their children were performing in the first phase. The practical assessment was administered towards the end of phase two, again to a sample of children.

In the third phase of the project, the number of teachers involved was doubled, as each of the original group identified a partner, usually from the same school, with whom they would work to attempt to pass on the strategies that phase two had found effective for improving science activities. This phase was preceded by a conference at which phase one and two teachers pooled and shared a number of strategies. Later these strategies were collated by team members and circulated for reference. While the teachers in the original group and those new to the project worked together in the third phase, the assessment instruments were used in the classes of the latter, but as much for their function in exemplifying the processes in action as for providing results about the children's performance.

From this outline of the STAR project it can be seen that the assessment instruments were to serve three purposes: summative in phase one, mainly formative in phase two and largely exemplification in the third phase. In order to do all of these things, as the TGAT report pointed out, the assessment procedures had to be capable of formative use, for the summative purpose could be served by aggregating across detailed results. Thus pupil assessment was designed so that it could give feedback on the performance of individual pupils and provide a useful exemplification of the process skills in action. It was also planned so that it could be used in classrooms with minimum interruption and intrusion into teaching and learning time. With the summative purpose in mind, it had to have built-in standard procedures so that it was sensible to add together results for individual children to look at performance of groups within and across classes.

The need for practical and written tasks

The question arises as to why two modes of assessment were thought necessary. The answer lies in the fact that no one form of assessment is ever completely adequate, and the shortcomings of any particular form depend on the nature of what is being assessed. The focus of the STAR assessment was children's development of science process skills (for reasons which will be given in the next section), and there are two intrinsic features of process skills which are relevant to this issue. The first is that process skills have to be used on some content: there has to be something to observe, something about which to raise questions or to plan investigations. The second is that the performance of some process skills has to be observed in action in order to be confident that they have been used and to judge the level of operation. If we rely on the end product of a task in which the process skill may have been used, there is some ambiguity about what really happened and what was assessed. Both of these are relevant to the decision to use a combination of written and practical tasks in the STAR project, and perhaps in any assessment of science.

The point about the subject matter in which process skills are used rests on evidence that this makes a considerable difference. From everyday experience we know that certain tasks are easier if the context is familiar to us than if it is strange. People involved in various sports are notoriously quick at calculating scores, angles, speeds, etc., which they may well find far more demanding in another context. Again, we observe more acutely and accurately when we know what it is important to notice, say, about a bird in order to identify it, or the sky to forecast changes in the weather. There seem to be two effects here, the influence of knowledge of the subject matter and the influence of the nature of the subject matter on a person's perception of the task. The latter operates even when knowledge of the subject matter does not actually enter into the task. For example, the problem of finding the residual target score in playing darts may seem difficult to someone who does not play, even though the arithmetic is well within his or her grasp. The reaction of 'I don't know anything about darts' influences the person's willingness to tackle the calculation, which actually requires no knowledge of the game.

There is ample evidence to show that both of these effects of subject matter operate when children are asked to observe, devise a fair test, interpret results and so on. The APU results revealed differences in performance of the same process skill according to the subject matter or context in which the skill has to be used (Russell et al., 1988, page 108). One important distinction in context is between problems set in an 'everyday' context, and those set in the more controlled classroom situation. Response to 'everyday' contexts tended to be in terms of 'everyday' reasoning rather than the more rigorous response to investigations in the classroom. But since science at the primary level attempts to blur this distinction by bringing many 'everyday' problems into the classroom, the reaction to a particular task could not be predicted.

One way of minimizing the effect of subject matter on children's performance of process-based tasks is to create a number of tasks with a range of different subject matter, so that the bias caused is averaged out. This was the approach adopted by the APU survey design, where it was possible because the surveys were concerned with reporting on the population and not on individual pupils. A large number of test items could be given across the sample, although each child was assessed in only a few items. In the classroom, the best way of assessing performance across a range of different subject matter is to collect information from normal classroom activities, in other words, continuous assessment by teachers. This was not an option open to the STAR project because of the purposes the assessment had to fulfil, as indicated above. As a compromise, an extended set of tasks was produced, each process skill being required in relation to different kinds of subject matter. It is, of course, far more feasible to provide this range in written tasks than in practical tasks, and so the 'Walled Garden' assessment was produced. This compendium of tasks, related to the exploration of an imaginary walled garden, was presented to children as a class project, which children could complete over a period of two or three weeks. It is described in detail in *Assessing Science in the Primary Classroom: Written Tasks* (Schilling *et al.*, 1990).

Thus the use of written tasks went some way to overcoming the problem caused by the effect of the context in which the assessment tasks are set. But on their own, written tasks would not give a sufficiently valid test of process skills. For one thing they do not provide information about the process skills **in action**, which was mentioned earlier as being necessary. While it is possible to create ingenious tasks (as in the Walled Garden) requiring children to do certain things and then record their answers, what is written is much less informative than observing how the activity is carried out.

Moreover, the written tasks have to be short ones, in order to cover many areas of subject matter, each focusing on a particular process skill. The question arises as to whether a child's performance on several short tasks of this kind adds up to the same thing as performance of the skills in combination, as in a whole investigation. The discussion on pages 4 and 5 about the pros and cons of discrete items as compared with whole investigations is relevant here. As both have advantages and disadvantages and there is evidence that the two are not the same, a combination is the obvious choice.

In summary, the STAR project used a number of short tasks, related to specific process skills and leading to a written response, in order to spread the assessment over a range of subject matter. It also used a practical activity which required process skills to be used in the context of a whole investigation, where performance was observed and interaction of observer and child could clarify the intention behind certain actions.

Reasons for the process focus of STAR

There were, and no doubt still are, many reasons for difficulties in teaching science in the primary school. Those mentioned in the 1978 HMI report included the lack of effective school programmes and policies for science; superficial teaching of science processes; insufficient attention to basic science concepts; inadequate background knowledge of teachers; poor match between the demand of activities and pupils' development in scientific skills and ideas. Any one of these could have been the subject of extensive research, for none had been systematically addressed at that time. However, since 1986, research has been carried out into some of these problems, notably the investigation of children's scientific concepts and how to promote these, by the SPACE (Science Processes and Concepts Exploration) project (Russell *et al.*, 1989) and the enquiry into the scientific understanding of teachers by Kruger and Summers (1988).

At the time that the STAR project was being planned, in 1984–5, the role of process skills in learning was under examination, prompted to some extent by the research into children's ideas in science (which at that time had been carried out mainly at secondary level). The recognition that children work out their own ideas about the physical and biological aspects of the world around them, and that these play an important part in learning, is central to the constructivist view of learning. This view gathered wide support from research in recent years, and is reflected in the Non-statutory Guidance to the National Curriculum in Science (NCC, 1989). In essence, it means that learning with understanding (as opposed to learning by rote) requires pupils to take an active part in constructing meaning from their observations and investigation of things around. It suggests that in trying to understand their experiences, children start from their existing ideas which they modify if necessary to take into account new evidence. This view of learning contrasts with the notion of children's minds being empty spaces into which new knowledge can be poured.

It is in enquiring further into the way in which children may modify their ideas in the light of new evidence that the role of process skills acquires importance (Harlen, 1985). An existing idea, which may be useful in attempting to explain something new, is brought to mind because of some perceived link with the new event or phenomenon. This link may arise from observing similarities and differences between the new and previous experience; or it may be created by two things having been encountered in the same place or at the same time; or by words which recall an earlier event. The usefulness of the linked idea in helping understanding of the new event has to be tested out against further evidence coming from exploration and investigation.

In both the linking of an idea to an event and the testing of it, processes such as observation, interpretation, question raising, hypothesis creating, prediction, the planning and carrying out of investigations and communication are used. If these processes are carried out scientifically, the result will indicate whether or not the initial idea was relevant and helpful, or whether it requires modification, or whether it ought to be rejected and some other idea used to suggest an explanation. In this way, concepts are gradually developed which are consistent with available experience.

However, the skills involved in carrying out these processes also develop slowly in children. At first, they will not be 'scientific': observation may be superficial and selective, so that only evidence confirming an idea is taken into account; predictions may be merely statements of what is already known rather than based on reasoning that 'if this . . . is the case then that . . . will happen'; tests may be carried out in ways which do not control effects other than the one which is being investigated; and so on. If these inadequacies are present in the processing of ideas and evidence, then ideas may well be accepted which should be rejected or vice versa. Thus the development of useful, scientific ideas depends on **how** the processes are carried out, that is, on the development of process skills.

This argument for the importance of process skills rests on their essential role in the development of understanding. It does not claim that process skills are to be developed because they have some intrinsic value – in terms of an abstraction such as for training a 'scientific mind', for instance – but because of their role in learning with understanding. Providing children with a richness of experience of the world around is not enough unless they engage with it in a way which uses and develops their process skills. The development of these skills is thus a high priority in improving learning in science.

It might be thought, however, that sufficient attention has already been given to processes in the curriculum materials available to teachers. After all, the emphasis of the Science 5/13 project, of the Nuffield Junior Science Project before it, and of some of the sets of materials developed in the late 1970s and early 1980s, is on process-based investigation. However, it was clear from the surveys of practice carried out at that time that these intended approaches did not become translated into practice. In some cases, physical activity replaced mental activity – children were busy 'doing', but on closer examination were seen to be following instructions and not thinking things out for themselves, and rarely were their ideas being tried out in the way which has been indicated in a 'constructivist' approach to learning. In real terms, there was gross neglect of children's process skills, despite the lip-service given to their importance.

Implicit in the points above is the notion that process skills can develop from less to more scientific forms, and that this development can be encouraged through the action of teachers. Even where this was recognized, though, there was difficulty in implementing it because the course of the development in process skills had not been researched to any extent. This was a further reason for selecting process skills as the focus of the STAR work, although it was not set up as a research specifically to map out the course of this development. Reference was made to work which has been done (mainly in the course of the APU surveys and some by Harlen *et al.*, 1977) in setting up an initial framework for describing development of process skills. Subsequent work in the project enabled this to be refined. Now development of these skills is explicitly embodied in the statements of attainment of Attainment Target 1 of the National Curriculum and we shall consider the relationship between the STAR formulation and the National Curriculum statements in the next chapter.

2

Development and Progression in Process Skills

THE STAR LIST OF PROCESS SKILLS

The process focus of the STAR project constituted a 'spine' which supported and unified the three kinds of assessment used: written tasks, practical activity and classroom observation. The same skills, defined in the same way and giving rise to the same criteria for assessment, were used throughout.

The choice of skills was based upon a pragmatic judgement as to the best way of expressing the meaning of the processes involved in linking and testing ideas, as described in the last chapter. Teachers were used to processes being expressed as separate skills in classroom materials (e.g. Science 5/13, Learning Through Science, Look!, Exploring) and in the HMI and DES reports and policy statements (e.g. DES, 1985, page 3) and in the APU assessment framework (Harlen et al 1984). These lists are not identical in the terms used to describe the process skills, but they all bear a strong resemblance to each other. Differences appear, for example, because of varying definitions of words such as 'predicting', which is sometimes, but not always, taken to be part of 'interpreting' (as in the APU framework), or again, whether separate parts of 'planning', such as 'controlling variables', are picked out.

With all lists of separate process skills, it is necessary to emphasize the warning that the identification of individual process skills does not imply or suggest that they are to be treated as having independent existence in practice. Rather they should be regarded as interdependent aspects of behaviour. It was with this understanding that the following skills were adopted as the spine process skills in the STAR project:

observing	planning investigations
interpreting	recording and communicating
hypothesizing	measuring
raising questions	critically reflecting

The list does not include 'investigating' or 'experimenting' because these are activities which bring together the identified skills; they are not separate process skills but composed from the ones listed.

The following brief description of these terms as adopted by the STAR project is given to fill out the overall picture before going into further detail, although the whole of this chapter is concerned with defining the character and development of these process skills.

Observing – using all the senses, as appropriate and safe, to gather information about things in the environment; sequencing and comparing events; noticing similarities and differences between objects and events.

Interpreting – bringing together information given or gathered so as to detect patterns or trends in it; to make predictions or inferences based on any perceived patterns, or draw conclusions.

Hypothesizing – proposing possible explanations of events or phenomena, particularly ones that can be tested by experiment; applying science concepts or ideas from previous experience to give alternative explanations that are consistent with the observed evidence.

Raising questions – posing questions that can be answered by observation or investigation or that can be turned into investigable questions.

Planning – identifying at least some of the steps and actions which have to be taken to solve a problem, to carry out an investigation or to collect evidence of certain kinds; recognizing the variables that have to be controlled or changed or measured for a fair and appropriate test to be made.

Measuring – quantifying observations so as to be able to say 'how much' using some non-standard or standard unit; choosing and using an appropriate instrument and degree of accuracy for measuring for a particular purpose.

Recording and communicating – making an oral or written report of observations, results, conclusions; expressing and being able to understand information in the form of graphs, charts, diagrams, etc., as well as prose.

Critically reflecting – looking back on earlier ideas or on what has been done in an investigation to suggest changes which would be improvements in future situations of the same kind; considering and evaluating alternative procedures and ideas.

RELATIONSHIP OF STAR PROCESS SKILLS TO THE NATIONAL CURRICULUM FOR SCIENCE

The National Curriculum was created some time after the STAR list was drawn up. The National Curriculum provides, in the form of Attainment Target 1, yet another set of process skills. These are described in different ways in the Programmes of Study and in the Statements of Attainment. For example, the Programme of Study for Key Stage 2 mentions that children's activities should involve them in controlling variables, solving problems qualitatively, but with increasing use of quantification; formulating hypotheses; using equipment and measurement; systematically recording; searching for patterns in data; interpretation and evaluation of data; oral and written reporting; and using a 'limited technical vocabulary'. Here all the process skills identified by STAR are explicitly included, apart from 'critically reflecting', although this may be implicit in 'evaluation of data'.

In the preamble to the Statements of Attainment for AT1 the skills are summarized as:

(1) plan, hypothesize and predict
(2) design and carry out investigations
(3) interpret results and findings
(4) draw inferences
(5) communicate exploratory tasks and experiments.

Surprisingly, this list omits 'observe', but it is clear that this skill is well represented in the Statements of Attainment. The relationship between the STAR process skills and the statements in AT1 for Levels 1 to 5 is indicated in Table 2.1.

Only one statement is omitted because it cannot readily be related to any of the items in the STAR list: 'carry out an investigation with due regard to safety'. There is also one item in the STAR list for which there is no related statement at Levels 1 to 5. In the National Curriculum, the first Statement of Attainment relating to

Table 2.1 *The science process skills in Levels 1 to 5 of the National Curriculum*

Process Skills	1	2	Level 3	4	5
Observing	1a	2b	3b, 3d	4e	
Interpreting		2e	3h	4i	5d
Hypothesising			3a	4b	5a
Raising questions		2a		4a	5a
Planning			3c	4c, 4d	5a, 5b, 5c
Measuring		2c	3e	4e	5c
Recording and communicating	1b	2d, 2f	3f, 3g, 3i	4f, 4h, 4j	5d
Critically reflecting					

critical reflection is at Level 6: 'produce reports which include a critical evaluation of certain features of the experiment, such as reliability, validity of measurements and experimental design'. However, as we have noted, there is indication in the Programme of Study for Key Stage 2 that some experience of 'evaluation of data against the demands of the problem' is expected.

Some of the National Curriculum Statements of Attainment have been slotted in at more than one place in Table 2.1. This applies particularly at Level 5 where the National Curriculum statements tend to imply the use of several process skills. This acknowledges that the combination of skills in practice, already mentioned, becomes particularly important as pupils become able to tackle more complex and extended investigations.

ASSESSING THE DEVELOPMENT OF PROCESS SKILLS

To assess the extent to which a child has developed a particular skill, it is necessary to have a clear notion of development. One way of conceiving development is as the accretion of more of the component sub-skills. This would mean identifying a number of sub-skills, not necessarily ordered in terms of supposed difficulty, and making the assumption that the more of these which can be carried out, the more the skill as a whole has been developed. For example, supposing that six sub-skills have been identified for a particular skill, then the child who performs three of them is considered more advanced than the child who performs only two, even though the two children may have achieved different sub-skills.

Another way of describing development is to try to identify as sub-skills, aspects of the skill which are progressively more demanding, so that there is a hierarchy in the sub-skills. In this approach, the intention would be to identify sub-skills such that a child who achieves three of them would have achieved the same ones as the child who achieves two, plus the next more difficult one in the order.

The second approach was adopted in the STAR practical assessment – the project set itself the task of describing skills in terms of progression. For each skill it identified five statements of progressive sophistication, using information available from research (particularly the APU results), and from trial work as a guide. The National Curriculum also describes progression in skills in the ten levels of the National Curriculum, and so the following description of the progressive development of the STAR skills makes reference to the statements of the National Curriculum to show the parallels in the development spelled out in the two cases. To the extent that these coincide, the work of the STAR project can help teachers to assess the process skills of their pupils by observing their practical activities as required for Teachers' Assessment of Attainment Target 1. The account of how this was done is taken up in Chapters 3, 4 and 5.

PROGRESSION IN OBSERVING

Observation is used in all areas of life, both out of school and within the school curriculum. It involves **using all the senses** and everything that is said here should be taken as applying to observation by touch, hearing, smelling and tasting (where safe and appropriate), as well as by sight. In science, observation is an important way of gathering information relevant to a problem or an investigation, and its meaning is more focused than in everyday usage. In this more closely defined view of observation, it is possible to identify changes that map out a dimension of progression.

One of the early signs of development is that children **notice greater detail than merely gross features.** Their attention to detail has to be inferred from their actions as a result of their observation, since we do not have direct access to their sense perception. What children say, draw, or write about what they see, smell, hear, taste or feel with their fingers is an important source of evidence of their observation. Attention needs to be paid to these signs because simply giving opportunity for observation of detail will not necessarily mean that it has taken place. A useful sign of attention to detail is the voluntary **use of some aid to careful observation,** such as a hand lens or stethoscope.

As their experience increases, it becomes possible for children to focus their observation on that **detail which is relevant to the problem.** Knowledge from previous experience is required in order to know what is likely to be relevant, a further acknowledgement of the influence of knowledge on process skills, noted in the last chapter. For example, it is not possible to eliminate the relevance of the colour of the plastic cover of a wire from its function in a simple circuit if you have never seen wires, bulbs and batteries before. Evidence that observation has taken place often shows in children being able to **identify differences between objects or**

Table 2.2 *The skill of observing*

STAR	AT1
Notices gross features of a phenomenon or object.	1a Observe familiar materials and events in their immediate environment, at first hand, using their senses.
Notice details of a phenomenon or object.	2b Identify simple differences.
Focus on observations relevant to a problem in hand.	3b Identify and describe simple variables that change over time.
Notice differences between similar objects or events.	3d Select and use simple instruments to enhance observations.
Notice similarities between different objects or events.	4e Select and use a range of measuring instruments, as appropriate, to quantify observations of physical quantities such as volume and temperature.

events that are similar. A related aspect is **detecting changes from one time to another**, since this means comparing the state of something at one time with the same object a little later, and this is important in many investigations. The use of **measurement in observation** indicates that relevant changes are being observed carefully.

The APU results suggested that noticing differences between similar objects or events is often rather easier than **identifying similarities between events and objects that are different from each other**. The latter involves making links between things, a process that plays an important part in the development of concepts.

The aspects of change that have been highlighted here sketch a path of progress as identified in the STAR project and in the National Curriculum for AT1. The two sets of statements are set out side by side, so that the extent to which they describe the same development in slightly different terms can be judged (see Table 2.2).

PROGRESSION IN INTERPRETING

Interpretation is a process concerned with using observations or data collected. Perhaps the first step in this process is when children **make use of all the evidence available** to them rather than using only preconceived ideas based on their experience. So the child who put some lettuce seedlings in a cupboard for a week to 'show' (in his words) that they would not grow so quickly as ones in daylight, was confronted with evidence which conflicted with his ideas (the ones in the cupboard did not look so green as the others, but they were taller). He reported that the ones in the cupboard were growing more quickly to get out, but at least he acknowledged the difference in growth rate.

Central to interpretation is **being able to relate one piece of evidence to another**; to see patterns of association of one thing with another. Some patterns are consistent across all the data – on a summer's day the position of a shadow will move steadily round in the same direction, for example. The association between the time and the position of the shadow is so regular that it can be used to predict the position of the shadow at any particular time. On the other hand, the length of the shadow will first decrease and then increase during the day, and so there is not such a simple relationship between shadow length and time of day.

In other cases, while there is a general trend, there is not an exact relationship. For example, if we measure the feet of people of different height, there is a general tendency for longer feet to be associated with greater height, but there will be some who have smaller feet than those who are taller than they are. Being able to identify overall relationships, despite the exceptions, is important in science, and depends on taking account of all the information available. This is something which children appear not to do at first. They tend rather to see the extremes – 'the tallest person has the longest feet' – and not look for the pattern across all the data. However, this is a first step in **recognizing that one factor may be associated with another**.

It is often difficult to know whether children who make a limited statement that seems to be only about part of the data have, in fact, noticed that all the data are related in the same way, but not felt it important to mention. Only when the statement explicitly embraces all the data can we be sure that **the interpretation is based on all the information that is available.** In this case, the statement is along the lines of 'the later the time, the further round the shadow is', or 'usually people have longer feet the taller they are'.

To be sure that there is a pattern linking one variable to another, at least three sets of observations are needed. Measuring the rate of growth of the lettuce seedlings in the cupboard and in the light is not enough to establish a pattern in the rate of growth and the amount of light. It would be necessary to have a third light condition and to see if the growth varied in the way expected if there were a relationship. It is important to check all suggested patterns in this way, by making a prediction based on the pattern and seeing if the reality fits the prediction. Thus **gathering further information to check interpretations** is a considerable advance in the skill of interpreting data. It also represents a step towards realizing that all relationships are tentative and always subject to being disproved by evidence, although this realization is unlikely to become conscious until very much later (it appears as a Statement of Attainment at Level 8 in Attainment Target 17).

Making predictions is presented here as part of the process of interpretation, intimately linked to establishing that a pattern or relationship between variables exists. Children do, however, make what they think are 'predictions', which may be anything from a wild guess to an idea arising from some preconception of what should happen. Actually, children seldom guess completely without some foundation; there is usually a germ of a reason based on evidence, though they may not be able to express it clearly. Being able to **explain a prediction in terms of the pattern on which it is based** indicates a grasp of the relationship and an advance in the process skill of deriving relationships from evidence.

Table 2.3   *The skill of interpreting*

STAR	AT1
Making interpretation related to data (rather than to preconceived ideas) even if only loosely.	2e Interpret findings by associating one factor with another.
Make interpretation based on all available data.	3h Interpret observations in terms of a generalized statement.
Check interpretation against new data.	4i Draw conclusions from experimental results. Base interpretation explicitly on pattern or relationship.
Interpretation explicitly based on pattern or relationship.	5d Make written statements of the patterns derived from the data obtained from various sources.
Justify prediction in terms of observed relationship.	

The threads of development picked out in the STAR project's description and those indicated in the National Curriculum statements of attainment are shown in Table 2.3 (page 21).

PROGRESSION IN MAKING HYPOTHESES

While interpretation is about using information to find patterns, draw conclusions and make predictions, hypothesizing is about trying to **explain** or account for data or observations. It involves **using concepts or knowledge from previous experience** and is one aspect of what is sometimes described as 'application' (as in the APU list of skill categories). Two important aspects make a hypothesis scientific. First it has to be **consistent with the evidence**; a hypothesis that a block of wood floats because it is light in weight but a coin sinks because it is heavy is inconsistent with the evidence if the block is heavier than the coin. Second, it has to be **testable** by collecting relevant evidence; the hypothesis about the block floating because of its weight is testable. If the suggested reason were that it is suspended from an invisible, immaterial and undetectable thread, then it would be untestable.

There may be several testable hypotheses consistent with evidence, as in attempting to explain why one kite will fly higher than another (tail length? weight? shape? area?), and testing by investigation may eliminate some or all of them. Even a hypothesis which is not eliminated is still not proved to be 'correct', for there is always the possibility that it could be disproved by further evidence not so far collected. There is never enough positive evidence to prove a hypothesis correct, but one (sound and reliable) negative test is enough to reject it. Thus a further characteristic of any hypothesis – any explanation – is that it is tentative and can be disproved.

Children do not naturally formulate hypotheses with these essential characteristics; but there is a gradual progression in this process skill towards this direction. Identifying a feature of an event or phenomenon **which is relevant to giving an explanation** is a first step, as for example, suggesting that what makes bicycle wheels go round is 'something to do with the chain'.

Connecting the phenomenon with a **relevant idea from previous experience** follows as the next step. Often this, as in the case of the earlier step, **may involve only giving a name to something**; not proposing any kind of mechanism that actually explains how it works or why something happens. For example, a stale slice of bread shrinks because it 'dries up'. This is hardly a testable hypothesis in the way described, but it is a foundation for further development.

The ability to **propose a mechanism** for the way a suggested explanation works is a necessary step in expressing a hypothesis in a way that is testable. If there is a mechanism that describes how one thing is supposed to relate to another, then this can be used to make a prediction. The evidence of whether the prediction is supported is then the test of the hypothesis on which it is based. If it is not disproved then it can be accepted, tentatively, as the best explanation pending further suggestions and evidence.

Children's ability to propose mechanisms is naturally limited by their experience and ideas. They may, on occasion, put forward a hypothesis which is not possible, although they do not know this to be the case. Alternatively, they may overlook what is to an adult an obvious explanation, because they have not yet access to the relevant concept. However, as long as the explanation is testable then we should see this as part of the development of the process of hypothesizing. With further experience, children will become more able to propose hypotheses that **fit the evidence and are consistent with science concepts.**

As their skill develops further, the recognition of the tentativeness of hypotheses will show in children being able to **give more than one possible explanation** that is consistent with evidence and science concepts. These explanations may not be proposed formally as 'I think this is the reason for . . .', but may be expressed in questions posed or investigations planned and undertaken. 'Will the colours spread more quickly if we use warm water?' (in simple chromatography) is a question which encompasses a hypothesis. 'Let's see if the water disappears if we cover the saucer with cling film' similarly arises from a suggested mechanism, in this case for the water disappearing from a saucer.

Again we can draw together the line of development in this skill identified in STAR and in the National Curriculum (Table 2.4).

Table 2.4 *The skill of hypothesizing*

STAR	AT1
Mention relevant features (at least) in attempting an explanation.	3a Formulate hypotheses.
	4b Formulate testable hypotheses.
Give an explanation in terms of a relevant concept (even if only by naming it).	5a Use concepts, knowledge and skills to suggest simple questions and design investigations to answer them.
Give an explanation in terms of a mechanism involving a concept (correct or incorrect).	
Give an explanation in terms of a mechanism which fits evidence and is consistent with science concepts.	
Give or acknowledge more than one explanation.	

PROGRESSION IN RAISING QUESTIONS

As we have just seen, there is some overlap between hypothesizing and raising questions. Some, but not all, questions are implicitly based on hypotheses and some, but not all, hypotheses can be expressed in terms of questions. However, apart from the way in which they may be expressed, there is a further similarity. In their more developed and scientific forms, they **lead to investigation or experimentation**. Raising questions as a science process skill is concerned with questions that can be answered by enquiry; at the primary level these are questions that children can answer by enquiry themselves, or that they know can be answered by enquiry.

Raising investigable questions is important, not just for the sake of being able to formulate and recognize such questions but, as in the case of all the process skills, because they lead to the children creating greater understanding of things around them. This understanding comes gradually through putting ideas and evidence together, prompted in the first instance by a desire to know, by a question. The clarity of the children's questions indicates the degree of their awareness of what they want to know and how it fits in with what they already know.

There are various degrees in specifying the kind of enquiry that is needed to answer a question. 'Is this kite bettr than that one?' is not strictly in an investigable form because it does not specify what 'best' means (although we can make a good guess). If the question is rephrased to specify that by 'best' we mean how high it flies, then it becomes clear what to look for (the dependent variable) to find the answer. In this case, it is already clear that what is being compared are two kites, and it is the type of kite that is to be changed in the investigation (the independent variable). It may well be possible to be more precise about what it is that is different about the two kites (such as the size, or length of tail, etc.) and so to identify an independent variable which is a variable feature of the kites rather than the whole of each one.

While the aim in development of question raising in science is to help children raise questions which are *investigable*, the starting point towards this is raising questions of any kind. To indicate too soon that science is concerned with certain kinds of questions and not others might deter the raising of any questions. So we should see **asking questions of any kind** as a first step to progress in this skill. These may be questions which ask for names, information, or explanations; they may be philosophical or ones which address aesthetic values; or they may be answerable by investigation or be capable of being turned into questions that can be investigated (see Jelly, 1985). By taking children's questions seriously so that they see for themselves how each kind is answered, and by posing questions in investigable form in science, teachers can help children to clarify their questions so that they can see how to find an answer.

Children will readily ask **questions in terms of 'how' and 'why'**, which are often not easy to answer: 'How do worms move without any legs?' 'Why are woodlice hard on the outside and soft in the middle?' In fact, these are **well on the way to being investigable** and it may take little more than an invitation to say, 'What do you think is the answer?', to set the children off on an investigation to see if their ideas fit the evidence. Once they see that they can find out an answer which satisfies them by being more specific in their questioning, they will begin to ask questions in investigable form, such as, 'Which of these foods do the caterpillars eat?' rather than 'What food do they like?'; or 'Will this toy truck move faster if . . .?' instead of 'Why won't this truck move any faster?'

When investigable questions are asked more frequently, it is likely to be because the children find them more effective, but without consciously identifying how they differ from questions of other kinds. Becoming aware that **some kinds of questions can be answered by investigation while other kinds cannot** is a point of progress. Once this difference is recognized, children may be able to go futher and **rephrase vague questions into a form so that they can be answered by investigation.**

Putting these ideas together in the STAR project led to the following description of progression, which can be compared with the statements relating to question raising at different levels of the National Curriculum.

Table 2.5   *The skill of raising questions*

STAR	AT1
Raise more than one question (any kind).	2a Ask questions and suggest ideas of the 'how', 'why' and 'what will happen if' variety.
Raise at least one question which is potentially investigable, although the dependent variable may not be specified.	
	4a Raise questions in a form that can be investigated.
Express at least one question in investigable form.	
	5a Use concepts, knowledge and skills to suggest simple questions, and design investigations to answer them.
Distinguish between a question which can be answered by investigation and other types.	
Reformulate a potentially investigable but vague question into one in which the independent variable and dependent variable are identified.	

PROGRESSION IN PLANNING INVESTIGATIONS

Planning an investigation is the process that turns a question or a hypothesis into action designed to provide an answer. Although logically it may be thought to precede action, in reality the two are often closely intertwined. Younger children, for example, may not be able to think through a series of actions that could be considered as a plan; they need to see what happens as a result of the first step they think of before working out what to do next. It takes experience of investigations, of doing things and seeing what happens, before the possible outcomes of action can be anticipated and forward planning becomes possible. Thus we can see the first step in planning as being able to **suggest an action that makes a relevant start on the solution of a problem or on an investigation**. This may mean, for example, in an investigation of the waterproofness of fabrics, no more than suggesting dropping water on the fabrics. The children might try this in a totally uncontrolled way and then, through discussion, realize that they need to think about how much water they should use, how to apply it to the fabrics (for 'fairness'), and how to judge the result.

As a way into considering variables, the notion of 'fairness' is a useful one. There are three kinds of variables to be considered in an investigation: the variable to change so that a difference between things or conditions can be investigated (this is the independent variable); the variables that must not be changed, but must be controlled and kept the same throughout so that the effect of changing the one independent variable can be investigated; the variable that is affected as a result of changing the independent variable and that is measured or compared in the investigation (the dependent variable).

In the common type of investigation represented by the comparison of fabrics for waterproofness, the type of fabric is the independent variable and the variables to be controlled depend on how the test is to be carried out. For example, if the fabrics are to be tested by placing water on the surface and seeing how long it takes to soak in, then it is important to use the same amount of water on each one and to apply it in the same way (two of the variables to be controlled). What is measured is the time taken for the drops to no longer stand on the surface. Alternatively, if the fabrics were compared by seeing how **much** water each will soak up, then it would be important to use the same area of fabric (a variable to be controlled); the dependent variable would be the amount of water in each piece, probably measured by the difference between the water added and what was left after soaking the fabric.

Not surprisingly, research and results from the APU surveys have shown that children find the earlier parts of an investigation the easiest to plan. They can decide **what to change – the independent variable** – quite readily because this is often clear in the hypothesis or question under investigation. 'Which is the best fabric . . .?' immediately suggests trying different fabrics. As soon as they begin to think of how to proceed with the investigation, however, the matter of fairness will arise. Several unfair tests may well have to be experienced before the understanding of **needing to control variables** develops in a general way. It is certainly best for children to realize through the inconclusiveness of 'unfair' testing that certain things have to be kept the same. In this way, the development of critical reflection (see page 31) is also aided. Attempts to teach control as a procedure often result in a tendency for children to think that they have to control everything, including the independent variable.

It seems that deciding on how to arrive at the result of an investigation is more difficult than planning how to set up conditions to test the independent variable. Children are at first very vague about how they will find a result in an investigation. For example, in testing food preferences of 'minibeasts' they think as far as 'see how they like each food' as if this would in some way be obvious. Ideas about measuring

Table 2.6 *The skill of planning investigations*

STAR	AT1
Identify starting point or initial actions relevant to the investigation.	3c Distinguish between a 'fair' and an 'unfair' test.
Identify appropriate variable to change or the things to be compared.	4c Construct 'fair tests'.
Identify at least one variable which should be kept the same for a fair test.	4d Plan an investigation where the plan indicates that the relevant variables have been identified and others controlled.
Identify all relevant variables to control for a fair test.	5a Use concepts, knowledge and skills to suggest simple questions and design investigations to answer them.
Identify an appropriate variable to measure or compare	5b Identify and manipulate relevant and dependent/independent variables, choosing appropriately between ranges, numbers and values.
	5c Select and use measuring instruments to quantify variables and use more complex measuring instruments with the required degree of accuracy.

time spent on the food, or amount eaten, come only when the impossibility of judging what small creatures 'like' is borne on them in practice. Thus **precision in identifying what to measure or compare** represents an advance in the process skill of planning. Further defining how to **measure the dependent variable to an appropriate degree of accuracy** is also a sign of this development.

The STAR description of progression starts with the early step mentioned above, while the National Curriculum introduces planning related skill in AT1 only at the point of beginning to recognize 'fairness'. The description of development can be compared in Table 2.6.

PROGRESSION IN MEASURING

One of the overall signs of progress in scientific investigation is the increased quantification of variables. Quantification means using numbers in a particular way. Numbers can be used merely as labels, as in the case of the numbers on the jerseys of football players, or as ways of placing objects in a sequence according to some feature or property, such as one being longer, shorter, hotter, faster, than the next. When the differences between one item and another are **quantified** it is possible to tell **how much** one thing is longer, shorter, hotter, faster than another and then relationships can be refined, patterns identified and predictions made from them.

The basis for saying 'how much' needs to be in terms of some uniform unit, but this need not be a standard unit. If children are introduced to measurement through standard procedures and units, they may be less likely to understand what a quantity actually means than if they can take the first steps by **using arbitrary or non-standard units** which they choose themselves – floor tiles for how far a wind up toy travels, bricks in a wall for comparing heights, hand spans, strides, etc. The understanding of the nature of a measurement as being a number of multiples of a given unit can be grasped in this way. It soon becomes obvious that there is a need to keep the unit the same, that is, to use the same brick wall to compare heights in terms of bricks; or have the same person striding over distances to be compared; and that a more convenient way is to use standard units such as metres, which mean the same everywhere.

Whether the unit is arbitrary or standard, it has to be appropriate to the size of the quantity being measured. It is inappropriate to measure the mass of a paper clip in kilograms or a person's height in miles. The choice of unit is tied to the instrument for measuring it, and experience of various instruments for measuring quantities of mass, time, length, volume and temperature has to be acquired for children to be able to **select an appropriate measuring instrument and use it with the degree of accuracy that is required.**

As the observations and relationships with which children become concerned become more detailed and precise, so the measurements they make need to be more accurate. Accuracy comes only partly from the skill of using a measuring instrument carefully; it also depends on the procedures adopted, such as how many different measurements are taken and how many times each measurement of the same thing is repeated.

Arranging to take an adequate set of measurements is part of planning an investigation, so that the range of variation in the independent variable is thoroughly investigated. For example, if the investigation is about the effect of temperature on how quickly substances dissolve, the result is unlikely to be conclusive if only cold and slightly warm water is used. A greater range of temperatures, and at least three different ones across this range, need to be used. Planning to **take measurements across an adequate range** indicates a development in understanding of the role of measurement in investigations.

Additionally, **the accuracy of each measurement has to be appropriate.** It is as unhelpful to measure something to a high degree of accuracy beyond that required, as it is to leave a great deal of uncertainty about the value because a measurement is rough. Accuracy can be improved to an extent by **careful use of instruments**, but this cannot avoid the inevitable errors that arise in investigations and are inherent in measurement. Recognizing, for example, that the time taken for a certain mass of a substance to dissolve at a particular temperature will not be exactly the same if the test is repeated, and that therefore **repeating measurements will reduce the error**, represents a quite sophisticated level of development of the process skill of

Table 2.7 *The skill of measuring*

STAR	AT1
Make comparisons in terms of some quantity which is measured or estimated.	2c Use non-standard and standard measures.
Use an appropriate unit of measurement, standard or arbitrary.	3e Quantify variables, as appropriate, to the nearest labelled divisions of simple measuring instruments.
Choose the quantity to measure or compare such that reasonable accuracy is possible.	4e Select and use a range of measuring instruments, as appropriate, to quantify observations of physical quantities such as volume and temperature.
Take an adequate set of measurements of the relevant variable.	
Check or repeat measurements to improve accuracy.	5c Select and use measuring instruments to quantify variables and use more complex measuring instruments with the required degree of accuracy.

measurement. Experience in the APU surveys shows that not many primary children repeat measurements routinely, and they are unlikely to realize that there is some error attached to any measurement however carefully it is made. However, they may begin to appreciate the uncertainty of measurements in situations where the chance of error is particularly obvious, as, for instance, in deciding exactly when a solid has completely dissolved.

From this discussion it is clear that there is a considerable knowledge base required for the development of the measurement skill; there are conventions and procedures of measurement that have to be known and the appropriate deployment of these is the basis of progression, as the statements proposed in STAR and in the National Curriculum show (Table 2.7).

PROGRESSION IN RECORDING AND COMMUNICATING

In common with observing and raising questions, recording and communicating are applicable right across the curriculum, and so their particular role in science has to be defined. These skills are included as science process skills because of their role in developing understanding of the world, in linking ideas to new events, in testing them, and particularly in reflecting on how these ideas relate to evidence gathered.

Recording and communicating are to be thought of in a far broader context than of producing a report at the end of an activity. Rather, both written and oral recording and communicating are integral parts of the activity throughout. Children need help in this, for at first they tend to make few records during an activity and inevitably are unable to recall all relevant observations afterwards.

The development of skill in the area of recording and communicating begins with a willingness to **talk about all aspects of observations and experiences.** Gradually, their experience and guidance from their teacher enable children to organize the reporting of their work in science by presenting similar observations together, sequencing events, and using simple charts, drawings and pictures to supplement words. Extending the range of modes of communication requires some knowledge of ways of presenting information and of the conventions of using them.

Table 2.8   *The skills of recording and communicating*

STAR	AT1
Make notes or drawings at the end of investigations.	1b Describe and communicate their observations, ideally through talking in groups or by other means, within their class.
Make notes or drawings during investigations.	
	2d List and collate observations.
Use tables or other standard framework for recording findings during an investigation.	2f Record findings in charts, drawings and other appropriate forms.
Provide a reasonably accurate oral account of actions and findings.	3f Record experimental findings, for example, in tables and bar charts.
Provide a reasonably accurate written account of actions and findings.	3g Interpret simple pictograms and bar charts.
	3i Describe activities carried out by sequencing the major events.
	4f Follow written instructions and diagrammatic representations.
	4h Record results by appropriate means, such as by simple tables, bar charts, line graphs.
	4j Describe investigations in the form of ordered prose, using a limited technical vocabulary.
	5d Make written statements of the pattern obtained from various sources.

Once introduced to the **use of forms such as block graphs, flow diagrams, symbols, keys, etc.**, the development of skill shows in **using these appropriately**.

Parallel with the increased use of graphical and written forms of communication is the continuing and important development of **using words**, in both **written and oral forms, with accuracy and selectivity**. Organizing a report so that **events are described in a useful order** becomes important when communication is genuinely used to inform others. Ensuring that there is some point in making a record, in the form of an audience for it, is a help in this respect. Since communication is two-way, reading or listening to others' reports helps in fostering clear expression, as well as being important in its own right for finding out about others' ideas and for contributing towards the **understanding of written information and instructions**. Written sources will increasingly be used for data, to supplement what is gathered at first hand, and the ability to interpret such data and search for patterns in it is an indication that the form in which it is presented is well understood.

A gradual increase in the meaningful use of scientific vocabulary is part of progression in the skills of recording and communicating. The use of specific scientific words is necessary since, as ideas become more advanced, they become more abstract and widely applicable; when referring to a solid in a liquid the word 'disappear' has to be replaced by 'dissolve' in order to cover the range of effects which may occur; 'vibration' must gradually replace 'move up and down' because vibration can be in all directions; and 'conductor' is a very useful word to describe the invisible property of all the different substances that allow electricity to flow through them. The introduction of a new word has, of course, to coincide with the development of the idea which it labels, for the use of technical words without meaning is an obstacle to communication. Table 2.8 summarises the STAR criteria and National Curriculum Statements.

PROGRESSION IN REFLECTING CRITICALLY

The meaning of critical reflection has to be confined to a role in scientific enquiry for the present purpose. In the STAR project, the term was used particularly in relation to children reviewing the procedures and ideas they used in their investigations. Much more can be learned from an activity if, after completing it, there is consideration of questions such as, 'Could we have used a different approach?', 'Should we have controlled other variables?', 'Did we need to measure that?', 'What other information should we have collected?' 'Have our ideas about what might be the cause changed?'

At early stages in scientific exploration, children tend not to ask these self-critical questions spontaneously; they have a strong urge to go on to do something else. Given encouragement and opportunity, perhaps at the end of a reporting and sharing session, children become more willing to **review what they have done**. Through this kind of review, talking over their work in an informal and non-threatening way, they become aware that details could have been changed. For example, that in their traffic survey they could have chosen a slightly different spot for observation which might have made it easier for them not to miss some of the

Table 2.9   *The skill of critical reflection*

STAR

Willing to review what has been done even if comments are only justificatory.

Admits the possibility of alternative approaches or features of the investigation.

Suggests ways of improving details of the investigations.

Considers pros and cons of alternative approaches or features.

Offers criticism of approach chosen or may start again with a different approach.

---

vehicles. An advance in reflection is shown when they realize that **there were alternative procedures and ideas that could have been used.** Perhaps their traffic survey should have been repeated at different times or on different days in order to test the ideas they had. Eventually, regular discussion after the event leads to children becoming **able to consider alternatives before the event in planning their investigations.**

Somewhat paradoxically, it is found that children who have devised quite effective procedures are more ready to criticize them than those who have gone about their investigations in less adequate ways. Thus, willingness to be self-critical does not mean that there is more to criticize; indeed, it may well be that the development of critical reflection helps the development of those skills which are the subject of critical review.

As there are no National Curriculum statements in levels 1 to 5 relating to this skill, we can only give the progressive statements for reflecting critically that were identified in the STAR project (Table 2.9).

3

The Water Sprinkler – a structured practical assessment

In order to obtain some indicators of children's competence with practical science activities in the STAR project, an assessment procedure had to be specially devised. This chapter describes how the instrument was designed to offer children the opportunity to demonstrate their expertise in all the relevant process skills and how the task was administered. It covers:

- the origins of the task in classroom activities;
- the development from the prototype to the final form;
- how the coverage of all the process skills was accomplished;
- the development of the administration procedure;
- the development of the marking and recording system.

CLASSROOM ORIGINS OF THE WATER SPRINKLER PRACTICAL TASK

The issue of the impact which the context of a task may have was raised in Chapter 1; it is not uncommon for people to define their own ability, or lack of it, by reference to the context alone. 'I'm no good at . . . mechanical problems, finding electrical faults, propagating plant cuttings', or whatever, is often heard from adults and children alike. (Worst of all, 'I'm no good at *science*.') These kinds of statements are frequently uttered with no consideration of the actual demand that is posed by the problem at hand. The mental set is in place, the prophecy of failure is waiting to be fulfilled. In a practical investigation, constraints of time determine that all skills have to be deployed within the scope of a single setting. Consequently, it is critically important that the context is engaging and acceptable to as wide a range of children as possible.

Familiarity of the **subject matter** is another important consideration. Children and adults may deny their ability to solve even simple logical problems such as syllogisms (Luria, 1976) if the **content** is unfamiliar. (One example of a syllogism presented to Soviet peasants started with the major premise, 'In the Far North where there is snow, all bears are white'; this was followed by a minor premise, 'Novaya Zemlya is in the Far North' and the question to be answered by simple deduction: 'What colour are bears there?' Many responses were to the effect that the respondent had never been to the Far North, knew nothing about bears and so was not in a position to answer the question.) The context of a task is important because it tends to limit the kind of content or subject matter which it is possible to introduce. If the subject matter is familiar, it is likely to be more accessible, meaningful or 'user friendly' – we feel able to 'get a handle on' the problem. Since children had already been involved in the written assessment, subject matter related to that same context was an obvious starting point for the development of a practical assessment activity.

The topic of watering plants arose as a natural consequence of children working on the 'Walled Garden' written assessment materials. Good assessment practices may have much in common with good classroom practice, and it is perfectly logical that the two should interact, one activity giving rise to ideas for use in the other; any interesting classroom activity is likely to generate further questions, and this is exactly what happened on this occasion. One class had turned its attention to the possibility of devising an automatic seed-tray sprinkler. It was from children's attempts to judge the relative effectiveness of a range of devices that they had constructed that the germ of the idea for the Water Sprinkler practical assessment procedure grew.

Many children's constructions worked on the principle of the rose of a watering can as the mechanism with which to generate a fine spray over a wide area. One of the more striking devices that children devised was a suspended plastic bottle with just two holes pierced in opposite sides of its base. The holes were covered by fingers while the bottle was being filled with water; when released, the jets of water caused the bottle to spin on the thread by which it was held, with the result that the water was distributed over a fairly wide area (Figure 4.1).

This was clearly an idea worth developing because it aroused such interested responses from children, from wide eyes to broad grins. There was also a clear science/technology basis to the activity, and apparent scope for developing the activity towards complete coverage of the process skills. However, as the activity stood, it was only a product, one solution to a problem-solving activity. The first step in its development as an assessment activity was to open up the task again in such a way that it might be presented to children as a fresh investigation. A practical assessment task must be reasonably 'open' in the sense of permitting more than one approach; if it is 'closed' to the extent that there is only one correct procedure, this will:

(1) have an inhibiting effect on children's performance, and
(2) preclude the collection of any performance information from all those children who do not proceed in the assumed direction.

On the other hand, the activity must be sufficiently defined to permit children's performance to be described against a common set of criteria. Thus, what started

Figure 4.1   *The Water Sprinkler.*

as a 'problem solving' activity was used as the basis for an enquiry which might be put into action by children in a number of different ways, but which could be assessed by reference to a common set of criteria.

The immediate issue was to identify a variable which would be reasonably evident to children as capable of being monitored. The spinning of the bottle was an obvious choice – it could be simply observed, or in the case of those children who recognized the relevance, it could also be measured. Another reason for feeling at an early stage that the activity had rich assessment potential was that there was a range of factors which could be adjusted to explore their effect on how the bottle might spin. These included:

- the length of the thread;
- the type of thread;
- the volume of liquid in the bottle;
- the type of liquid used;

- the size, number and positioning of the holes;
- the dimensions of the bottle.

There was also plenty of scope for standard and non-standard measurements to be taken, while the situation also seemed to be capable of engaging children possessing little or nothing in the way of measurement skills. Quantification might involve:

- number (rotations of the bottle);
- time (duration of the spinning movement);
- length (of the string);
- volume (of the water).

Although it might not be expected very often if at all, there was also the potential for children to combine their measurements of time and number of rotations to produce a measure of **rate**, the number of turns in a given time.

Once data are collected, it is possible to summarize and interpret them. Thus, opportunities for recording and interpreting were also clearly available.

It would also be possible to explore children's conceptual understanding by inviting them to generate hypotheses to account for the spinning motion, action and reaction of forces, elasticity of the thread and perhaps ideas about gravity.

DEVELOPMENT OF THE PROTOTYPE

There was a point in the development of the Water Sprinkler activity at which it was almost abandoned. The attraction of the activity, that which causes it to surprise and delight, is the action-reaction event – the way in which the jets of water cause the bottle to spin. The jets arc and trail in graceful curves which spring out and then wane as the water level falls. Unfortunately (as it seemed initially), the **empty** bottle, instead of coming to rest and signalling a neat end to the event, begins to start spinning in the reverse direction. The decision was taken to work with the event instead of against it; the counter-spinning could be incorporated as part of the focus of the investigation. This would also help to guarantee that the required investigation was a novel one for all children participating, as it was most unlikely that any would have explored the spinning in both directions.

The next step in the development of the protocol was to resolve various practical details. A collection of plastic flasks with flattened front and back faces was obtained; a sufficient number of the same type of bottle meant that the task could be presented in a standard form to each child by a number of interviewers. Compared with round bottles the flat bottles also demonstrated the spinning phenomenon particularly well. A durable thread was found in kite string. The fabrication of simple wire hooks and hangers took much of the practical awkwardness and uncertainty out of the task. (One prototype bottle was suspended, filled with water and, before release, the child's prediction of what would happen was invited. The response volunteered was that the bottle would 'fall down'. Even before the interviewer could frame a response to this sceptic, the prediction was devastatingly confirmed!) A task which is designed to be standardized, as this one was, must have reliable equipment.

Development of the prototype continued by inviting a number of children to attempt the investigation, one at a time. In this way, the exact wording to be used could be developed to an unambiguous form and wrinkles in the procedure ironed out. For example, to fill the bottle with water while blocking the holes requires two pairs of hands. It was decided that the interviewer should offer assistance, under the child's direction. In practice, interviewers had to be alert to the possibility of being unwittingly switched into the role of the investigator – an outcome that some children tried to engineer!

GROUP OR INDIVIDUAL ASSESSMENT

During the development of the task, there was some exploration of the possibility of assessing a group of two or three children at once. The outcome for the interviewer was rather like being given directions by two or more people simultaneously – they may see different landmarks as salient as well as using different ways of saying the same thing. What tended to happen in practice was that one child would do the explaining while the others gave way. In the classroom situation, this need not be a problem because the views of the less forceful children can be canvassed at another time, or on another occasion. It is important to see the development of this practical task within the STAR project and the use of practical assessment as a **classroom** technique as imposing two different constraints. In a 'one-off' project interview, assessment information on each child being assessed has to be obtained against every criterion; there is only one opportunity to do so. In the classroom, the teacher can use similar assessment structures as children work in a range of different contexts, over time. In this way, the profile of performance for each child can gradually be assembled. The time constraints of the project required a complete profile from each child interviewed from a single session, and this seems best accomplished by having the children working one at a time.

The performance criteria against which children's actions were to be assessed had already been established (see Chapter 2). The initial pilot trials revealed:

- how those general process skill criteria could be formulated in specific form in the Water Sprinkler task;
- what gaps in the coverage of the process skills remained to be filled by means of the design of supplementary activities.

The pilot activities generated ideas for filling the various gaps as well as suggesting a workable order of presentation of the task. As a result, an **administration procedure** was formalized. It consisted of an inventory of apparatus, a sequence of sub-routines and a loosely-worded script and set of instructions for interviewers. All of these were designed to produce a standardized interview schedule that would allow comparison of children's performance. A **coding sheet** for recording children's responses and a pupil **response sheet** which included the wording of the investigation as it was posed, with space for any recording which children chose to make, completed the documentation. (See Appendices Ia, Ib and Ic).

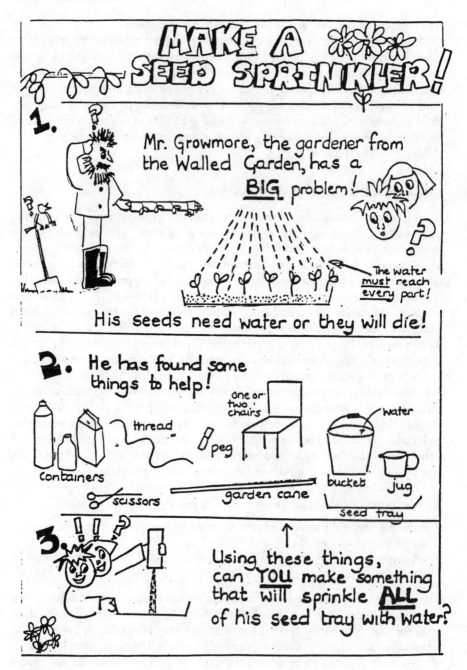

Figure 3.2   *The classroom poster introducing the seed sprinkler problem.*

THE ADMINISTRATION PROCEDURE

The administration of the practical assessment can be thought of as unfolding in four phases:

(1) classroom familiarization;
(2) interview discussion prior to the investigation;
(3) the investigation itself, conducted by the child;
(4) post-interview discussion.

The **pre-interview classroom familiarization** consisted of a period of time devoted to setting the context of the problem for children. This was to ensure that they did not meet the task 'cold'. A poster setting the context – the need for a seed tray sprinkler – was put on the classroom wall and children were given about two weeks to look at it, think about the problem, discuss it with others and perhaps try out some ideas (Figure 3.2). Various equipment was suggested, including plastic bottles, thread, buckets, polythene sheeting, etc. (It was left to children to think of measuring equipment.) Teachers were asked to encourage children to have a go at the problem during any spare moments, by themselves, without any assistance from the teacher.

The **discussion prior to the investigation** was part of the one-to-one session during which a relaxed and informal climate was developed. This also provided the opportunity to talk about any activities that had been carried out in the classroom prior to the interview. Evidence of **critical reflection** on any sprinkler development activities in which the child had engaged, or in which other children had been seen to engage could be collected at this point. As the task equipment was introduced (see Figure 3.3), there was opportunity for an **observation** task: two bottles in which holes had been pierced (at different heights from the base, different sizes and different relative positions) were offered for comparison of similarities and differences. The phenomenon of the spinning bottle was also introduced at this point: the interviewer covered the holes at the base of the bottle and invited the child to pour water into it; the bottle was then suspended by its hanger on the hook at the end of the thread and released. Questioning about what the child had seen to happen served to establish awareness of the phenomenon to be investigated and also provided another opportunity for **observation** to be assessed, but at a different level.

The **investigation** as conducted by the child was the core of the assessment procedure. During this phase, the child was given control of all the equipment and decisions about how it should be used to address the problem as posed:

Does the bottle spin as much after it's emptied as it did when the water was coming out?

The meaning of this question was clarified with the child in a very concrete manner, by moving the apparatus and by movements of the hands. How that question was put into operation, how it was turned into a practical investigation, was the child's own decision. During the course of the investigation, the interviewer collected evidence of the child's *recording* and any *measurement* that was undertaken. There was also discussion of the **interpretation** of any observations made or data collected.

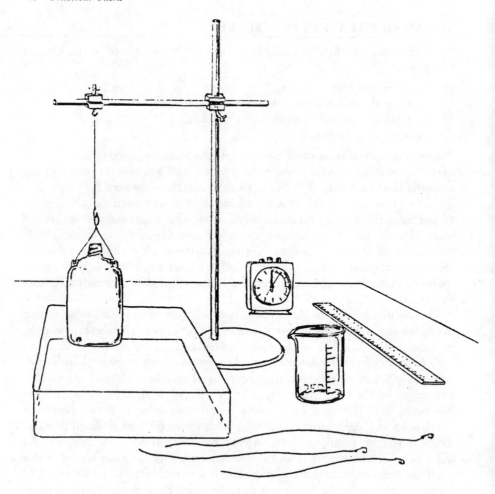

Figure 3.3   *Apparatus presented to children for the Water Sprinkler task.*

Post-investigation discussion provided the opportunity to go back over some of the ground covered during the investigation. This allowed **planning** decisions to be made explicit rather than simply inferred by the interviewer; children were encouraged to explain why certain things had been done in a particular way. During this part of the interview, various supplementary issues were raised so as to ensure a complete coverage of the process skills. For example, a summary of data 'collected by other children' allowed some questions about data **interpretation** to be posed, even in those cases in which children had not themselves collected sufficient data for a pattern to be evident. Questions about how the task might have been tackled differently revealed any **critical reflection;** discussion of the particular reasons for the bottle spinning in the way it had elicited **hypothesizing;** a discussion of how the apparatus might be used to explore other variables offered opportunities for **raising questions;** examination of the non-task bottle provided opportunity for further

hypothesizing to be explored. (The holes in the non-task bottle were smaller, further from the side and higher from the base; most importantly, they were opposite one another so that, in theory, the reaction forces of the jets of water might be assumed to cancel one another out).

It was considered important that these supplementary questions were all posed within the same context. Setting a completely new context – for example, with data about cars and ramps, or plant growth – and ensuring that a child understood it, would be a very inefficient and time-consuming way of proceeding, especially in a classroom situation. The organization described above maximizes the assessment opportunities by elaborating from a central core of activity, which, in its simplest form, can be described as a relationship between two variables. This relationship in action between an independent and a dependent variable is the irreducible minimum within any practical investigation.

The administration procedure with its elaborations around-the-central activity is reproduced in full on pages 100–105. On the left of each page will be found the general instructions and any specific wording used to ensure a standardized procedure. It was intended that the interview sequence should flow as naturally as possible within the structured framework; administrators were advised to use hand movements to make their meanings about the rotations of the bottle clear. On the right of the pages, adjacent to the procedural details, are the process skill references, the numbers one to five referring to the STAR criteria under consideration. A running sequence of numbers, 1–65, refers to each assessed point in the interview.

It will be noticed that there was more than one opportunity to assess some skills. Children were judged to have succeeded at a particular level if they met the criterion for success on **any** occasion.

THE MARKING AND RECORDING SYSTEM

The performance against each check-point was recorded for every pupil, using a simple binary system – each criterion was judged to have been achieved or not achieved. A coding sheet was designed to be aligned with the check-list on the right-hand side of the administration procedure notes. Each check point at which the child met the criterion was shaded.

During a practical assessment interview, there is always a great deal for the administrator to make sense of, to observe and to record, and a lot of paperwork to shuffle in what tended to be, in this instance, a rather damp environment! Any device which simplifies the administration is to be welcomed. As administrators became familiar with the procedure, it was usually possible to keep a written record of children's responses, thus amplifying the all-or-nothing scoring system with a more detailed qualitative record. Initially, it was found helpful to have an audio-recording of the interview so that any responses which raised doubt as to whether or not a criterion had been met might be considered and discussed at leisure. With practice and familiarity, it was possible to dispense with the audio-recording and record everything on the spot. Audio-recordings became redundant as interviewers became more clear about what they were looking for, which in turn gave them more time to observe each child's performance closely and accurately.

It will be noticed that some of the check-points have arrows referring back to the preceding level. This indicates that success at the higher level logically implies success at the lower level. Since the levels were designed to be hierarchical, it might be assumed that this would always be the case. In practice, whether or not children's performance formed a scale or hierarchy is an empirical question; it was always possible for children's performance to be uneven, in the sense that their spread of success was slightly unpredictable. The hierarchies might be less apparent for individuals than when performance is averaged for a group of children.

The next chapter examines in detail what children did in the situation which has been described, and exemplifies the nature of the performance which was elicited for each of the levels of each of the skills within the STAR definitions. The relationship between these descriptions and the requirements of the National Curriculum Statements of Attainment is also discussed.

4

A Summary of Performance on the Water Sprinkler Task

The previous chapter described the administrative details of the Water Sprinkler task and how it was designed to assess process skills. This chapter will exemplify the behaviours that were taken as evidence of children having met the range of STAR criteria within each of the skills assessed. Descriptions of how children performed will include the kinds of things children said and did, and what nature of response was accepted as meeting a particular defined criterion.

In considering the examples of children's responses, the various **purposes** of assessment as described in Chapter 1 should be borne in mind. There are several ways of looking at the products of children's practical activities, all of which are valid and have their uses, depending on a teacher's purposes. One use of such products is to construct qualitative impressions of individual children's performance against certain criteria in order to see their needs. This diagnostic information will help the teacher to make decisions about further appropriate learning experiences. The fine detail of what individuals did during the Water Sprinkler task provides this sort of information.

In the following pages, within each skill definition, the range of responses offered by children will be discussed in detail. This will serve to highlight the various demands of the tasks, help to clarify the skill definitions, and most likely reveal insights as to how progression within a particular skill occurs. At this point in the evolution of the National Curriculum and its assessment procedures, teachers have a particular need for **exemplification** of different kinds of pupil behaviour representative of different levels of performance. Criterion-referenced assessment is still an unfamiliar obligation to many teachers. Translating Statements of Attainment into what children actually do is a novel demand; the detailed appraisal of responses to the Water Sprinkler task should serve to help to unravel process skill demands and their interpretation.

THE SAMPLE

At the start of the STAR project, about twelve teachers were involved from each of the LEAs of Cheshire, Leicestershire, Sheffield and Wirral, with approximately equal representation of each authority. Most of the teachers were from different schools, but some teachers were paired within a school. All were teachers of Key Stage 2 children, ranging from year three to year six; a preference for the involvement of year five and year six children had been expressed, since the project planned to use some written assessment material which would necessarily be better suited to children who were likely to be reading at around the average eight-year-old level. In the event, some of the participating teachers had vertically grouped classes, while others taught younger groups in successive years of the project's duration. Consequently, the age span of the children involved ranged from year three to year six.

The administration of the Water Sprinkler assessments was carried out by members of the research teams, including the advisory teachers who worked very closely with the project. Each administrator was trained in the task procedure in order to standardize details, such as the amount of help that was permissible, acceptable supplementary questioning, etc. Practice sessions with volunteer pupils were observed; video recordings were analysed and discussed to clarify procedures and interpretations. Gradually, a set of records illustrating responses meeting the various criteria was compiled. This could be referred to whenever the administrator was in any doubt as to whether or not the criterion had been met by a particular form of response.

Since the practical assessment took about forty-five minutes (and sometimes longer), only six children from each class were involved. The sample was identical to that used for the classroom observation assessment (Cavendish *et al.*, 1990) and the Walled Garden written assessment tasks (Schilling *et al.*, 1990). Since a reasonably representative sample of children was needed to ensure that a valid picture of performance was drawn, children were selected using a randomized allocation system. (The project did not wish to assess only those children who would shine, nor those whom teachers thought might benefit from some individual attention outside the classroom!) Without indulging in too much soul-searching, teachers were asked to allocate all children in their class to one of three **achievement** bands by reference to their performance in class, across all areas of the curriculum. Using a random procedure, researchers selected one boy and one girl from each of these bands to represent each class, six children in all per class.

Analysis of performance over the three years of the project indicated that fairly stable measures were being achieved. The qualitative details of performance used to illustrate this chapter are drawn from the several hundred practical assessments which took place over the three years of the project. Since the concern here is with the **quality** of résponse, the ages of the children whose work or comments are reproduced are not specified. (Normative aspects of performance in relation to year six children are discussed in Chapter 5.)

THE QUALITY OF CHILDREN'S PERFORMANCE

Each of the science process skills will be discussed in turn in this section. The order of presentation will be that in which the skills first occurred in the practical interview. As indicated in Chapter 2, there is often a fairly close correspondence between the STAR progression and National Curriculum expectations. Where STAR project progressive skill levels are being exemplified, they will be labelled as such, using the first letter of the skill. For example, 'STAR H.3' refers to the third descriptor in the STAR Hypothesizing progression.

Since teachers' current concerns are with making sense of and putting into practice the National Curriculum, discussion of the different qualities of response given by children will also be used, where possible, to illustrate the process-based Statements of Attainment. Such exemplification will be referenced using the notation 'Sc 1', followed by a number representing the Statement of Attainment level, and a letter referring to the particular attribute within that level. For example, Sc 1/4b refers to the second criterion at level four, 'formulate testable hypotheses'.

CRITICAL REFLECTION

The assessment began with a discussion of any prior work carried out in the classroom. As well as breaking the ice, this served to give an indication of the extent to which children were able or willing to reflect critically on their activities. As indicated earlier, the National Curriculum does not refer to Critical Reflection within Levels 1 to 5; the Star project did explore children's performance in this area.

Children were asked to reflect on:

(1) attempts to develop a sprinkler in the classroom and
(2) the way in whick they had carried out their own practical investigation during the interview.

Without any negative overtones, they were asked whether there might be any way in which their procedure might have been modified in such a way as to improve the performance or the results.

In attempting to assess Critical Reflection, it must be borne in mind that young children tend to be egocentric – aware of only their own perspective. Science can be a creative activity, but its products and procedures must also have social credibility. Children have to learn to attempt to distance themselves from their own viewpoint to some extent, to try to be objective rather than only emotionally committed to a particular view. The assessment of the extent to which children are able to reflect dispassionately on their own performance is really only possible in the context of a discussion.

The delicacy of this area of self-criticism, the fact that it is so closely related to a sense of personal identity and well-being, which is in turn rooted in family and social development, as highlighted by the following poignant comment:

I didn't have a go. I don't know how. My friends asked me to make one, but I was no good. I've been trying to make one but my dad doesn't let me. He doesn't let me use any of his tools any more. I've tried to get at them but my dad kept on telling me off.

Figures 4.1 to 4.3   *Examples of children's Water Sprinkler designs.*

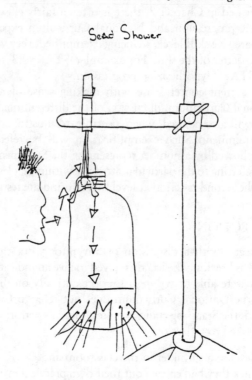

Sead Shower

Figure 4.1

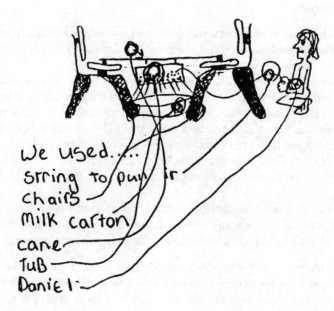

We used....
string to pull ir
chairs
milk carton
cane
TuB
Daniel

Figure 4.2

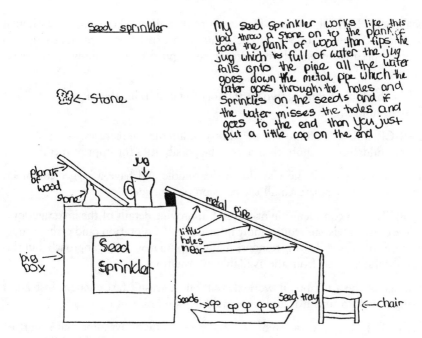

Figure 4.3

(Such a response would be credited at STAR CR.1, since, although a protestation of failure, there has been an attempt to review what has been done.)

The classroom activities provide an interesting example of the ways in which science and design/technology may interact, with children's designs incorporating their assumptions about scientific principles. As might be expected, children's attempts to design a sprinkler were very imaginative (see Figures 4.1–4.3). Almost without exception, design ideas are likely to raise further questions. For example, many of the designs for **automatic** devices were in effect extremely labour intensive, far more so than a watering can in most cases! Yet these attempts have value. They have engaged children's thinking about how things work, about levers, pulleys, remote control systems, gravity. Figure 4.1 in particular also raises issues of conceptual understanding. Does this child assume that blowing increases the pressure and causes the water to escape more quickly?

Many children could offer no suggestions for improving their sprinkler device. Sometimes this was because they were satisfied with their design. For example, Michael thought carefully about the possibility of improvements to his design:

> Get a bottle with holes in it. Put a hose on the end, connect it to the tap and turn the tap on.

(Since the comments are only justificatory, this is treated as a STAR CR.1 response.)

More frequently, children could suggest no improvements because they had not thought very clearly about the effectiveness of their device. For example, although their construction was supposed to be an **automatic** sprinkler, explicit attempts to reduce the need for personal involvement, as implied by the following response, were rare:

> We're thinking of joining two bottles together and fixing the sticks, so we don't have to hold it.

(STAR CR.2 since it admits the possibility of alternative features.)

Some children were quite clear about the possibilities for improvement:

> I could put holes all the way down the middle and have a bigger container, because it might not reach all the parts on the outside.

(STAR CR.3 – a consideration of ways of improving details of the investigation.)

More drastic revisions require more information/exploration (and perhaps more courage, also). The following response might imply a new design approach, but this is not absolutely clear from the available information:

> On one of the attempts, it worked well, but it wasn't fast enough. Instead of using a stick to turn it round, you could use a whisk to turn it.

(STAR CR.4 – a consideration of pros and cons of alternative approaches. Further probing and discussion might reveal a willingness on the part of this child to start over again with a new approach. This would constitute STAR CR.5, and implies a maturity and self confidence in outlook in approaching investigations and design problems.)

Having expended some time and effort on their investigations, children's comments often reflected satisfaction with their procedure. Many were prepared to consider some detailed changes in procedure, but suggestions for completely new approaches were rare.

OBSERVING

Although part of the practical activity throughout, there were two particular opportunities provided for the assessment of observing. The first occasion was before the investigation, when two plastic bottles were provided for comparison. Later, a dynamic situation was provided by the rotation of the suspended bottle (Figure 4.4).

Children were asked to compare the task and non-task bottles for similarities and differences. The bottle used in the investigation was fitted with a wire hanger; the small holes were punched on opposite sides, front and rear. The non-task bottle had no hanger; the holes were both on the same side of the bottles, were larger, higher from the base and further from the sides.

STAR O.1 criterion was met by children referring to just one gross feature of the set-up, and virtually any accurate observation was acceptable. For example, many children mentioned that the water was coming out, or that the bottle was spinning. Some children – a small minority – actually omitted to mention (or failed to

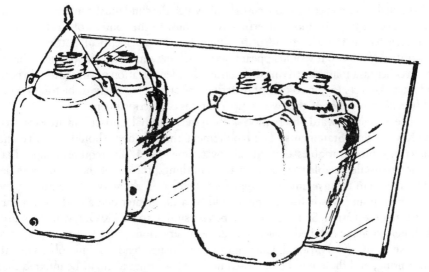

Figure 4.4   *The plastic bottles.*

observe) that the bottle changed the direction of spinning once it was empty.

The spinning of the bottle as the water jetted out offered the opportunity for children to comment on **sequences** of events: the graduated speeding and then slowing; the turning in one direction and then the other; the gradually increasing and then diminishing radius of the water as it hit the tray. This type of more detailed observation was accepted for STAR O.2:

> It started to speed up again, going the other way, once all the water was out.

> It twirls round and spreads the water all over the container – it does it quickly, it slows down, then it turns the other way and goes faster when its emptied.

Or:

> Its a thick spray. As it gets slower, the spray moves move into the middle of the tray.

This can be contrasted with a STAR O.1 response offering far less detail and conveying far less information:

> The bottle spins, the water's coming out. The water's gone everywhere.

STAR O.4 and O.5 respectively were concerned with the observation of at least two differences and two similarities. Most children indicated the colour, size and shape of the bottles as being similar, while the differing size and position of the holes was also noticed fairly readily. It should be noted that, depending on the subject matter under consideration, children usually seem to find it easier to notice differences than similarities. In this instance, the bottles shared **identical** rather than **similar** features; more often, the features which objects have in common may be underlying rather than on the surface. The implication is that they have to be

abstracted by reference to a conceptual link which the child must construct, whereas differences tend to be more superficially obvious. In the context of the Sprinkler, children found it easier to identify similarities in the identical bottles than to identify differences. It would appear that identifying similarities in identical objects is an easier task than identifying differences; the identification of similarities in non-identical objects (e.g. two cats of differing appearance) is likely to be found more difficult than either of the two comparison tasks described here.

The straightforward observation skills in the National Curriculum are expressed as Key Stage 1 Statements. The requirement that children should 'identify and describe simple variables that change over time' (Sc 1/3b) requires simply that children should be able to observe changes in things; the use of the word 'variable' does not seem to have any particular force here, as in the sense of identifying the variables in an investigation. This would be a far greater demand than straight-forward observation. Sc 1/3b seems to be very similar to STAR O.2, which requires children to make detailed rather than gross observations.

Several of the National Curriculum Statements tend to link observing to measuring, and these will be discussed under Measuring; it might be inferred that the National Curriculum promotes the bringing of simple instruments into the process of observing at a fairly early stage, certainly within Key Stage 1.

INTERPRETING

A major obstacle to the practical assessment of data interpretation is that children may not collect sufficient or reliable enough data to allow a trend to be revealed. A way around this is to provide them with data which has been obtained from a source other than their own investigations, but set in the same context. To provide data from an entirely different context would make the task different and more difficult. The data should be connected to the problem, materials and variables made familiar by the child's own attempts at an investigation. The task of interpreting the presented data can then focus immediately on the nature of the pattern in the results.

Prior to the Sprinkler interviews, data had been collected about how the bottle emptied when the length of the string by which it was suspended was varied. This resulted in the data summarized in Figure 4.5; for use in the interview, real lengths of thread were pasted to a sheet of A2 card in order to make the representation of the data as clear and direct as possible.

It was possible to assess the first two levels of interpreting from the investigation which each child carried out during the interview.

The bottle with the water in it goes fastest

(STAR I.1 – the interpretation of the data was related to the information presented, but no observations or comparisons had been made to justify the particular interpretation offered.)

When it goes the other way it twizzles faster and longer than when its full.

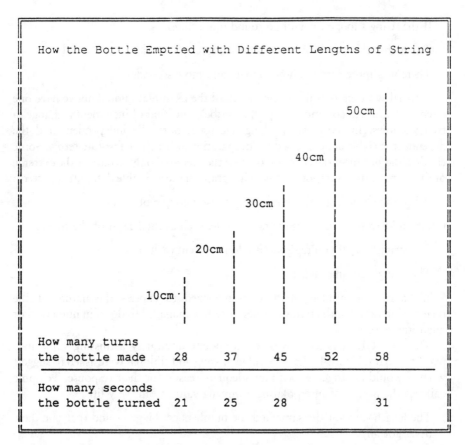

```
How the Bottle Emptied with Different Lengths of String
```

Figure 4.5   *Table of data presented to children for interpreting.*

(STAR I.2 – this interpretation integrates all the observations of spinning in both directions which the child had made.)

Since the higher levels of interpreting required a more precise description of a pattern or numerical relationship, the data shown in Figure 4.5 were used for reference. It can be seen that the context is the same in general as that in which the child has just attempted an investigation: the activity summarized on the chart should have been made more accessible as a result; all that has changed is the independent variable, the length of thread used to suspend the bottle. The dependent variable is expressed in two ways; number of turns and number of seconds. This was an attempt to increase the possibility of children making sense of the data in terms of the way in which they might have tackled their own investigation – how they put the dependent variable into operational form. The kinds of summary statements resulting were as follows:

When the string gets longer, the bottle turns more.

The bigger it gets, the more turns it does.

If the string's longer, it will go round more times.

The higher the length of the string the more spins it does.

There was more turns as it got longer and more seconds.

The actual wording was not critical, but all the examples quoted above have one essential feature in common: they all describe some kind of incremental change in two variables. In terms of the language used, both the independent and the dependent variable are expressed in **comparative** rather than **absolute** terms. Some children did not meet the criterion because they referred only to data at the extreme of the pattern; such a response fails to integrate all the available data into a pattern:

When the string's small it could only twist a couple of times.

Other children focused on only one variable, such as the length of the string:

The string . . . all you're doing is adding 10 cm each time.

The string's getting longer.

While a certain number of children managed to express the nature of the relationship between the two variables, very few managed to do so in numerical or quantitative terms.

The STAR I.5 challenge was to interpolate accurately a missing value in a pattern of data. Figure 4.5 has one value missing and children were asked to suggest what it would be, together with an adequate reason for their response. To some children the notion of interpolating a missing value meant very little:

The lengths are not the same and the numbers get bigger – and that one there never got any.

Interpreting in the National Curriculum is first indicated at Level 2 where children are required to 'interpret findings by associating one factor with another' (Sc1/2e). This seems to imply that children are required to infer a relationship between two variables, the 'factors' referred to being in effect the independent and the dependent variables in any investigation. For example, height of ramp and the distance a car rolls, length of string and amount the bottle turns. 'Associating one factor with another' might have the following qualities:

- the recognition of the existence of a connection between two variables – length of string 'has something to do with' the way the bottle turns;
- the recognition of a **causal direction** in the association, without necessarily an awareness of the nature of the relationship, 'the bottle turned most when the string was longest';
- the integration of all the information into an overall pattern, i.e. the **higher** the ramp, the **further** the car rolls.

Sc 1/2e would seem to call on at least the first of these qualities, and probably the second also. The next Statement in the National Curriculum, Sc 1/3h, 'interpret observations in terms of a generalized statement' seems to require the third quality, in which all the information is integrated into a general statement.

The next two references to Interpreting in the SoAs reflect the distinction between data patterns which children collect themselves and those which they derive from other sources.

Sc 1/4i requires that children 'draw conclusions from experimental results'. The implication seems to be that children must draw conclusions from data which they have themselves collected.

Sc 1/5d appears to demand something different – children must 'make written statements of the patterns derived from the data obtained from various sources'. Children are most likely to be involved in the collection of data which represents a **direct** relationship, i.e. as one thing increases, so does another. Sc 1/5d is perhaps a reminder that there are many other kinds of relationship which may be revealed by a set of data. For example, in an **inverse** pattern, as one thing increases, another decreases. There are also more complex patterns in which the relationship between an independent and dependent variable take the form of a **curve** when plotted, rather than a straight line.

For example, objects do not fall towards the Earth at a constant rate, but at a constantly increasing (accelerating) rate. Other relationships show a 'waxing and waning' pattern; an example is the length of shadow cast by a sundial which is longest in the early morning, is at its shortest at midday and gradually lengthens again until sunset. Such a range of different relationships and patterns might be found in a variety of sources, not necessarily those which children encounter at first hand. It is also true to say that interpreting the more complex patterns imposes a greater level of difficulty (Russell *et al.*, 1988); furthermore, the fact that these must be assessed as 'written statements' is likely to increase the burden on language skills.

RECORDING

Given the particular nature of the task, the recording opportunities in the Water Sprinkler investigation were limited. The factor which was of interest was simply whether the child made any notes or drawings **during** the investigation (STAR R.2), or only at the end (STAR R.1). In longer term or more comprehensive investigations, it would be expected that the assessment of recording and presentation of results might encompass data handling skills, including the use of tables and graphs. Such representations carry the implication that the investigation has been quantified and that measurements have been taken. In the Water Sprinkler set up, many children did not take any measurements, so, for them, tables and graphs were not even on the agenda. In those instances in which children did take measurements, they tended to record these immediately, so meeting the criterion for STAR R.2:

woterin3ʃ sec
Water out .117sec

The Bottle does spin more when it is emptied. I filled the bottle up and doe) let as It go. I als o started to time I found out that the bottle span round for 36 seconds with water in and 1.17 seconds without any water in.

Other children were satisfied with a much more limited recording in which they simply wrote their conclusions:

yes it does spin as much when it is emptied.

Within the National Curriculum SoAs, Recording and Communicating is represented by ten SoAs at Levels 1 and 2. This is no doubt indicative of the importance attached to the skill which is probably the most obviously cross-curricular aspect of science. The first requirement is at Level 1, where children should 'describe and communicate their observations, ideally through talking in groups or through other means, within their class'. This kind of activity, in which children attempt to articulate their observations, is a very familiar one even in reception classrooms.

The potential variety of forms of recording information and communicating it to others is recognized in the National Curriculum Statements. Sc 1/2d, 'list and collate observations', corresponds most closely to what was required in the Water Sprinkler task. The word 'collate' implies that there should be some sort of organization which might be seen as the first approach to the use of co-ordinate forms (tables, charts and graphs in which the vertical and horizontal axes can be used to read off particular values). The 'appropriate forms' in which it is suggested that findings should be recorded in Sc 1/2f are likely to be the products of the investigations themselves in a form which can be displayed. For example, outlines of size of feet of different numbers of children could be cut-outs; the distance cars roll might be shown as paint trails, and so on (see Figure 6.5).

Sc 1/3f refers to more conventional forms including tables and bar charts, while Sc 1/3g is a reminder that these forms have to be **interpreted** or read, as well as constructed.

Sc 1/3i is fairly unambiguous, being concerned with the skill of describing or reporting activities in sequence; Sc 1/4f describes the complementary skill of following written or diagrammatic instructions.

Sc 1/4h is probably more problematic, for as well as the use of tables and bar charts, children are expected, when 'appropriate', to use line graphs. The important point to bear in mind here is that the shift from the use of bar charts to the use of line graphs implies a considerable difference in performance and understanding. The kinds of variables which teachers encourage younger children to consider tend to be categories – colour, favourite food, type of transport, etc. Children may then count how many in each category are associated with particular groups. Categories are relatively sharply defined groups, which do not vary continuously. In the context of the Water Sprinkler task, relevant **categories** which might be used could include **type of bottle, kind of string, king of liquid**.

Only things that can be quantified or measured can be thought of as varying continuously – **height, mass, temperature, area**, etc. The reason this is important is that only those variables which vary continuously can be plotted as line graphs. The ability of children to handle continuous functions in line graphs might be separated by several years from their ability to use categories of data in bar charts. The wording of Sc 1/4h perhaps veils the fact that, within the statement itself, a range of acceptable outcomes is implied, probably spanning several years of development, rather than a single, fixed criterion.

Sc 1/4j requires that children should be able to 'describe investigations in the form of ordered prose, using a limited technical vocabulary'. The impression was gained from the Water Sprinkler task that many children were able to manage this, though frequently such notes were offered in the absence of a more structured record of quantified results. It seemed that children were using the less science-specific skill of recording in prose form at the expense of the more economical tabular record (see example above).

Sc 1/5d is included under Recording, as there is a communication element, but the interpreting skill is undoubtedly the greater demand; this Statement is therefore discussed under Interpreting (see page 53).

MEASURING

The Water Sprinkler task provided children with ample opportunity to display their measurement skills in action. They might measure the length of string used to suspend the bottle; they might choose to time the duration of rotation in a single direction or count the number of turns in a given time period; the volume of water which they poured into the bottle could also be measured. Although no instructions to take any measures were given, a ruler, measuring containers and a stopclock were provided. Each piece of apparatus was introduced and children were asked whether they knew how to use the stopclock. When they indicated that they did not, its function was demonstrated. Such demonstrations appeared to have little influence on the decision as to whether or not to use the stopclock in any subsequent investigation.

STAR M.1 required that children should make comparisons in terms of some quantity which is measured or estimated. If children attempted to quantify time at all – that is, if they tried to use the stopclock or the measuring vessel – they were deemed to have met this criterion.

STAR M.2 looked for the use of an appropriate unit of measurement, whether standard or arbitrary. In the absence of a stopclock, children might resort to counting to a pre-arranged number to fix a duration; some children adopted this strategy in preference to using the clock. In their attempts to standardize the amount of water which was poured into the bottle without resorting to measurement scales, some children used one or more whole beakers of water. Others overfilled the bottle so that it held water up to the brim to ensure that they were using the same amount each time.

STAR M.3 requires children to choose a quantity to measure or compare such that reasonable accuracy is possible. For example, reasonable accuracy could not possibly be achieved by a child who attempted to measure the time taken for one rotation of the bottle.

STAR M.4 is about taking an adequate **set of measurements** of the relevant variable. An example related to the particular investigation would be children measuring both the time the bottle took to empty, **and** the time it took to come to a halt after spinning in the reverse direction. This did cause many children problems if they resorted to stopping the clock in order to take a reading once the bottle had emptied, rather than making a mental note and allowing the clock to keep running. A set of measurements in this instance was liberally interpreted as consisting of a minimum of one measurement of spinning in each direction.

STAR M.5 calls for the checking or repeating of measurements to improve accuracy. In the case of ephemeral events such as the time taken by the bottle to empty, the action would need to be repeated; other types of measurement, such as volume or length may be easily checked without a complete re-run. Almost without exception, the Water Sprinkler investigation procedure was repeated only when children felt that they did not have a result, rather than to check or confirm what might have been an acceptable result.

The impression was that in using measurement, children tended to operate in an 'everyday' frame of thinking, where accuracy, replicability, certainty and proof of evidence are not the usual criteria. Children's measurement was generally sufficient to satisfy themselves; in science, an important function of measurement is actually to satisfy others with hard evidence.

The first mention of measurement skills in the National Curriculum occurs in Sc 1/2c, where children are required to 'use non-standard and standard measures'. The implication seems to be that any kind of measurement behaviour at all will satisfy this criterion, since it is known that the particular physical property (i.e., temperature, mass, length, etc.) has such a profound impact on performance. Furthermore, the particular scale graduation used will have an important bearing on the accuracy – and hence the difficulty level – of any measurements taken.

Sc 1/3e confirms that quantification is sought at an early point in children's scientific experience within the National Curriculum, children being required to quantify variables to the nearest labelled divisions. This Statement does not imply that children have to make decisions about **what** to quantify themselves, and it seems likely that many children in the infant phase will need guidance from their teachers in this respect. The available evidence suggests that children currently find decisions about how to quantify their investigations a challenge well into the primary school. This was certainly the case in the Water Sprinkler context.

Sc 1/4e is explicit that children must 'select and use' appropriate instruments for appropriate physical quantities; the implication is that this is the child's own decision within the context of an investigation. The example physical quantities referred to are volume and temperature. Sc 1/5c looks for development of the same skill with 'more complex measuring instruments with the required degree of accuracy'. The inference may be drawn that it is the nature of the investigation that determines the degree of accuracy required; this may prove to be the subject of debate on occasions, for, as mentioned above, children's inclination seems to be to measure sufficiently accurately to satisfy themselves rather than to satisfy any more external or objective criterion.

HYPOTHESIZING

Children were invited to offer explanations for three related phenomena. The first was why the bottle behaved as it did when the water was coming out, and responses were categorized according to the STAR H.1 to H.4 criteria.

The scientific explanation in this case is described by Newton's law that for every action there is an equal and opposite reaction. Water leaves the bottle through the small holes in the base under the force of gravity and the pressure of the 'head' of water in the bottle. The reaction in this case is the force acting on the bottle in an opposite direction to the jet of water. (This action-reaction phenomenon can be experienced by jumping off a stationary roundabout; this causes the roundabout to spin in the opposite direction to the jump.) Although the two jets are on opposite sides of the bottle, they both cause the bottle to spin around its vertical axis. As the water level decreases, the spinning slows, because the pressure of water is decreasing. Meanwhile, the thread is being twisted. When all the water has escaped, the energy stored in the twisted thread is released as the bottle begins to spin in the reverse direction.

Children were not expected to offer anything like such a formal explanation, but it was anticipated that they would attempt to use some related concepts.

STAR H.1 (Relevant feature mentioned):

When it comes out . . . the water makes it heavier . . . and when it gets lighter, so it can turn more easily.

The 'relevant feature' here is that the spinning is perceived as something to do with the water coming out of the bottle.

STAR H.2 (Gives an explanation in terms of a relevant concept):

I don't know. Is the string . . .? Because the water's coming out of both holes and making it turn round. Like a windmill. It's just water making the bottle go round.

The water and spinning are more specifically linked and an analogy, not entirely accurate, is drawn.

STAR H.3 (Explanation in terms of mechanism, whether correct or incorrect mechanism):

> The pressure of the water is making it go round, because of the water power. There's air in the bottle as well, it's pushing.

This response is partially correct (reference to the 'pressure' of the water), but air pressure is in fact equal inside and outside the bottle, so is not a relevant factor.

STAR H.4 (Explanation [mechanism] which fits the evidence and is consistent with science concepts):

> The water is pushing itself out on both sides and the force is making the bottle turn round.

Although slightly tangled in its wording, this description contains the elements of forces acting on the bottle from two sides.

Children were also invited to explain why the bottle turned in the reverse direction once it was empty, and responses were categorized in a manner similar to that described above.

Towards the end of the interview, the non-task bottle was examined and children were asked to suggest how it would behave if filled with water, suspended and released in the manner of the task bottle. In this case, the holes were smaller, nearer the centre, further from the base and, most importantly, both on the same side of the bottle. In theory, the two jets of water would be acting in opposite directions so that the forces of reaction should cancel one another out. (In practice, the less than perfect alignment of the holes would be likely to produce some sort of rotation.)

The STAR H.5 response required children to accept more than one **alternative** explanation, a very challenging criterion for most children in the primary age range. Children in this age group seem to prefer certainties; to hold two or more similar explanations open as possibilities would be evidence of mature and flexible reasoning.

Hypothesizing is a process in which the relationship between processes and concepts (which always exists to some degree) is strongest, since it calls on experience and understanding as much as it is enhanced by knowledge of procedures.

Hypothesizing in the National Curriculum is introduced as a Sc 1/3a, which simply requires that children should 'formulate hypotheses'. There is no specific requirement that children should always be right in their formulations, and at Level 3, it is most unlikely that they would be. On the other hand, since there are no other qualifications to the statement, it might be assumed that to meet this criterion, the hypotheses should have some bearing on the phenomenon under consideration. The distinction here is between hypotheses which posit a mechanism which may be incorrect (STAR H.3), and those in which the explanation fits the evidence and is consistent with science concepts (STAR H.4). In purely normative terms, in view of children's relative lack of scientific knowledge at Level 3, inaccurate but worthy attempts at explanations are likely to outnumber hypotheses that both fit the evidence **and** are consistent with science concepts.

Sc 1/4b requires not only that children should formulate hypotheses, but also that those hypotheses in theory be testable; these twin demands combine what were treated as two separate skills in STAR terms, i.e. Hypothesizing and Raising Questions. The implication of Sc 1/4b is that there has to be some correspondence between the theoretical and the practical – what children think is happening, and how it might be demonstrated that their hypothesis is correct (or incorrect). At Level 4, this is only likely to be the outcome with relatively simple and explicit mechanisms.

While Sc 1/4b states only that the testable hypothesis is to be 'formulated' (not necessarily tested), Sc 1/5a explicitly states that children must 'use concepts, knowledge and skills to suggest simple questions and design investigations to answer them'. In effect, this statement encompasses a complete practical investigation cycle, and, once again, the context of the task will have a critical bearing on whether it is within the scope of children to complete it. Sc 1/5a is discussed further under Raising Questions.

PLANNING

To assess planning, children were asked to review what they had been trying to do within the framework of the Water Sprinkler investigation which they had just conducted. Although much of their thinking was self-evident from their actions, by recounting what they had been trying to achieve, their purposes were clarified or confirmed. A second opportunity to assess their planning skills was provided in the context of the data relating the length of string by which the bottle was suspended to the way it would spin; children were asked how they would investigate this effect. The protocol enabled the interviewer to probe as to why certain things were suggested, what would be controlled, and so on. The following responses illustrate the different levels of response that were encountered:

STAR P.1 (Initial actions relevant to the investigation):

Attach the string and see how many times it goes round.

STAR P.2 (Identifies appropriate variable to change or things to compare);

Then you could attach it again with all the different pieces of string, 10 cm, 20 cm, 30 cm, and have a chart like this.

STAR P.3 – identifies at least one variable which should be kept the same for a fair test):

Put the same amount of water in each one.

The string? Make sure it was the same thickness.

I'd give a certain seconds or minutes. Do them all about three minutes.

Those children who are less familiar with the idea of a fair test in science often assume the everyday version of fair as 'just' or 'above board':

Set it up – someone could test it to see if I was right.

This type of response is not strictly a control, nor a repeated measure in the scientific sense, for the intention is to check the integrity of the investigator rather than the accuracy of the procedure.

STAR P.4 (Identifies all relevant variables to control for a fair test).

Any two variables from the following were accepted – type of thread, bottle, volume of water, size and position of holes.

STAR P.5 (Identifies appropriate variable to measure or compare).

Time them, see how long they take to slow down.

Put the water in the bottle, see how many turns the bottle made, then get another piece and see if the answer is the same difference.

The first reference to Planning in the SoAs is Sc 1/3c in which children must 'distinguish between a 'fair' and an 'unfair' test'. It is undoubtedly easier for children to spot weaknesses in someone else's design than it is to construct a fair test from scratch. One device used by teachers at Key Stage 1 is to make deliberate errors that may be spotted by children; if children show awareness of fairness in such a situation, they would appear to have met this criterion, though as mentioned earlier, children may tend to interpret fairness in the sense of social justice.

Sc 1/4c is quite clear in its requirement that children should construct their own fair tests, and this particular statement appears to be aimed at control variables specifically, rather than the plan of the investigation as a whole. The evidence for this conclusion is that the next SoA, Sc 1/4d, includes the planning of the independent and dependent variables: 'plan an investigation where the plan indicates that the relevant variables have been identified and others controlled'.

Sc 1/5a has been briefly discussed under Hypothesizing; the added dimension to the planning process that this SoA demands is the initial conceptual issue that is to be tested, for the planning must 'use concepts knowledge and skills'.

The next elaboration of the planning criteria is in the area of quantification. Sc 1/5b requires that children 'identify and manipulate relevant independent and dependent variables, choosing appropriately between ranges, values and numbers'; clearly, measurement of some kind is demanded if this criterion is to be met, but only at an 'appropriate' level – appropriate to the investigation, it must be assumed. Sc 1/5c extends the degree of precision in requiring children to 'select and use measuring instruments to quantify variables and use more complex measuring instruments with the required degree of accuracy'. 'Required' must be assumed to refer to the requirements of the investigation rather than the requirements of the child or teacher. For example, in timing the spinning bottle, attempts to time one spin of the bottle were bound to be inaccurate, so that Sc 1/5c would not have been met by such a strategy.

RAISING QUESTIONS

Turning ideas into investigations is possibly the most important thing which children have to learn to do in Profile Component 1 in the science curriculum. It is also an area in which teachers frequently expressed doubts as to how to help children.

The STAR hierarchy of skills under Raising Questions starts with the assumption that any sort of curiosity is to be encouraged initially, and this spirit of enquiry should gradually become more focused into the raising of investigable questions. It might be assumed that every child would have at least one question to raise, but in the event, some children responded with comments rather than questions. For example:

> You could just make a watering can. Use a plastic orange container with a string handle. Punch holes in it with a screwdriver or something.

The following responses illustrate the different levels of questions that children proposed.

STAR RQ.1 (Raises more than one question of any kind, not necessarily investigable):

> Find out how deep the deep end is in the swimming pool. Put that at the side of the pool (i.e. the stand) and see how deep the bottle goes.

This response was intriguing in that it had virtually no connection with the context under discussion, and yet managed to use the apparatus by improvising the bottle on a thread as a plumb line; however, it is a question and it does reveal a sense of curiosity!

STAR RQ.2 (Raises at least one question which is potentially investigable, though the dependent variable may not be specified):

> If it had a big hole in, would it come out fast, or would it come out slow?

There is no suggestion as to what would be taken to be 'fast' or 'slow'; the dependent variable is not specified in operational form, though the independent variable is clear and no doubt this child would be able to carry out an investigation of some sort, probably deciding how to deal with comparing rate of flow along the way.

STAR RQ.3 (Expresses at least one question in investigable form, independent and dependent variable stated):

> See how long it would take with bigger or smaller holes.

This proposed investigation is fairly explicit, but might benefit from a question from the teacher which asks the child to specify how holes of different sizes would be achieved.

STAR RQ.4 (Distinguishes, when requested, between a question which can be answered by investigation and other types). Three statements were introduced in printed form and read out to each child. The statements and some of the responses they evoked were as follows:

(1) Does the colour of the bottles make any difference to how they spin? Could this be answered by doing an investigation?

Get two or three bottles and paint them different colours, or if you have some [bottles of] different colours. Use the same amount of water and let them go at the same time and see which one twizzles the fastest or the slowest, and things.

I wouldn't have thought colour made any difference, but you could do an investigation – use different coloured bottles, the same string and amount of water and time them.

You could, but I don't think the colour would make any difference. It doesn't really matter about colour. Maybe if the container had a thicker layer of colour, and it was heavier, it would change the result.

Depends if you've got different colours of bottles. If so, yes. It wouldn't make any difference, a colour is a colour. Its not really gonna make that much difference.

(2) Why do we have pink bottles? Could this be answered by doing an investigation?

Yes, you could. Write to a factory – quite a few – and see why they do use them.

When questioned whether such an enquiry would constitute an investigation, this child replied:

Writing is investigating something. You're doing work on it. Writing is investigating. You could go out looking in bottle banks and see what labels they have on them.

No. It could be any reason. We could have any colour bottles.

No. I don't know. I don't think so . . . It's just like saying, 'Why do we have green bottles?', it doesn't make no difference.

They tell you what colour stuff is inside the bottles.

(This child simply offered information in response to the invitation to consider whether the statement could be investigated; this may be symptomatic of a relative unfamiliarity with the notion of finding things out through an investigation.)

(3) What would happen if the bottles were round and not flat? Could this be answered by doing an investigation?

Yes. Just get a round bottle and hook it on. But it might not be the same size. You'd find a bottle the same size.

Just test them, a flat and a round one, and see what was best.

They'd fall over and smash if they were glass.

STAR RQ.5 (Can reformulate a potentially investigable but vague question into one in which the IV and DV are identified):

Get two or three different types of string and do the same experiment, but keeping everything else the same.

Test thick ones, thin ones, different kinds. You'd have to have the same length every time. Just do the same – see how many times it turns.

Turning to the demands on Raising Questions within the National Curriculum, Sc 1/2a indicates that pupils should 'ask questions of the "how", "why" and "what will happen if" variety'. This opens a fairly broad range of possibilities. Children demonstrating a focused and relevant curiosity might be expected to show such behaviour fairly readily, since as expressed, it is not particularly science-specific behaviour which is required, though the context might be expected to be broadly science-based.

Sc 1/4a, separated by two Levels from the previous SoA in this area, imposes the added demand that children should 'raise questions in a form which can be investigated'. This demand seems identical to STAR RQ.3, illustrated above.

Sc 1/5a contains complex demands relevant to Hypothesizing and Planning as well as to Raising Questions; the implication is that the question should be completely thought out into some form of investigation which actually addresses the conceptual issue implied by the question, and gathers relevant information of a confirmatory (or disconfirmatory) nature. This is as far as any child could be expected to extend their understanding of investigatory science in the primary school (and, indeed, doubtless the same would be true for many pupils in the secondary phase also).

SUMMARY

The nature and range of children's responses to the Water Sprinkler practical assessment task have been detailed in this chapter. A similar range may be anticipated in other contexts based on other subject matter used in the classroom. Additionally, the National Curriculum criteria have been discussed in terms of what teachers might expect children to do in meeting the various Statements of Attainment. All criteria have to be interpreted in terms of specific examples, and these examples should as far as possible be derived from good practice in primary classrooms. What children are capable of achieving as they and their teachers become more familiar with the implementation of the science curriculum is a fascinating open question.

The next chapter will consider outcomes on the same Water Sprinkler task, but from the perspective of overall group levels of performance.

5

A Summary of Performance Across the Process Skills

The previous chapter described the range and quality of children's performance on the various component process skills exemplified by the Water Sprinkler task. This chapter turns to a consideration of the performance of year six children as a group, with a view to examining the overall strengths and weaknesses which may be inferred from their performance. **Quantitative** descriptions will take the form of percentage rates of success of year six girls and boys separately and combined. The relevance of such a quantified approach to the classroom teacher, referring as it does to measured levels of performance of a group, is that group measures of performance enable the teacher to be aware of the profile of performance of the group against the complete spectrum of skills. This information might prove to be diagnostically useful at the whole class level, especially if it produces surprises by revealing particular 'peaks' (which will give teachers pleasure and satisfaction), and 'troughs' (which will suggest that certain skills need some further development).

To complete the picture, characteristic approaches to investigations are also reported in the form of case histories. These brief cameos have been selected to illustrate how different component skills drawn from the whole spectrum of process skills combine to produce particular qualities of performance that define a child's approach. These descriptions should serve as a reminder that, in practice, the different levels and qualities of skill described are linked and integrated within an individual's performance. Undoubtedly, similar components of performances can be identified by teachers in their own classrooms, despite differences in the context of the particular science investigations with which children are likely to be engaged.

THE PERFORMANCE OF YEAR SIX CHILDREN ON THE WATER SPRINKLER TASK

Where percentage rates of success are quoted, these are based on data collected from 58 boys and 56 girls in 1988 and 1989. Results are reported for each check-point in the Water Sprinkler protocol in Appendix 1a; in the following pages, the same performance data are presented – but in aggregated form referring to STAR process criteria – in order to describe overall performance in each of the process skills as defined by the STAR project.

As described earlier, some skills were represented by more than one check-point in the interview. To gain credit at a particular STAR criterion, success on any occasion was accepted; showing a capability on any occasion rather than demonstrating complete **consistency** of performance was the standard which was applied. In the context of National Curriculum assessment, it will be necessary to be absolutely clear about this issue of consistency of performance in assessment. It is of great concern to teachers that children's performance (especially that of younger children) is, as often as not, variable. Children often appear to 'know' something on one occasion but not on another. This variability of performance need not in itself be a source of great concern – it is a fact of life. It is uncertainty about how to apply the assessment criteria in the face of such inconsistency that may generate anxiety. Assessment practice must always resolve such ambiguity by being quite specific about precisely what manner of performance is being assessed and reported. In the case of the STAR practical assessment, it was felt that children should be given as many opportunities as possible within the constraints of the Water Sprinkler task to show what they were capable of doing; in practice, the interview occasionally provided only one opportunity for children to use a particular skill.

It will be noticed that not all of the STAR levels produce results in practice which confirm the theoretical hierarchy of the criteria. For example, the overall level of performance for CR.5 is much higher than for CR.4, though in theory, CR.5 is assumed to pose a greater challenge. The criteria were constructed to make sense educationally and developmentally. The Water Sprinkler task gathered data to match against those criteria and, not too surprisingly, there are some apparent discrepancies. The acid test of the criteria is not whether or not they form perfect scales of difficulty, but their practical utility for examining children's science performance closely and analytically. It also has to be borne in mind that a different context matched to different performance indicators embedded in a different subject matter would almost certainly produce variations in absolute performance (i.e., the percentage level of success) and possibly in relative performance on the different levels also. The following paragraphs should be judged in terms of the insights they provide about children's performances against the specific challenges with which they were confronted.

Four-fifths of year six children interviewed (Table 5.1) demonstrated a willingness to review either the the classroom exploration of a sprinkler design, or the investigation that they undertook during the interview. Like most of the STAR first level criteria, this one is relatively undemanding; it might almost seem surprising that not all children were prepared to review their performance, if only in justificatory terms.

Against all the other criteria within this skill, children's performances were around or below the 50 per cent level, with the exception of CR.4, which required them to consider the 'pros and cons' of alternative approaches or features. Only 7

Table 5.1 *Critical reflection*

Task	STAR criteria	Per cent success year six children		
		Boys $n = 58$	Girls $n = 56$	All $n = 114$
Reflect on classroom attempts to construct a seed sprinkler.	CR.1 Willing to review what has been done, even if comments are only justificatory.	89	88	88
Reflect on actual investigation conducted into spinning bottle.	CR.2 Admits the possibility of alternative approaches or features of investigation.	40	48	44
	CR.3 Suggests ways of improving details of the investigation.	49	52	51
	CR.4 Consider pros and cons of alternative approaches or features.	11	3	7
	CR.5 Offers criticism of approach chosen or may start again with a different approach.	34	49	42

per cent of children overall managed to offer appropriate suggestions. It is possible that the Water Sprinkler task offers a relatively narrow range of options to children in this regard. On the other hand, almost half of the sample were able either to criticize their own approach, or put such an implicit criticism into action by starting again with a different approach.

CR.5 shows a significantly higher performance by boys than girls. This difference is accounted for by performance on check-point 31 (see Appendix 1b), where children were asked to review their investigation with the interviewer. Boys were assessed as being more likely to countenance a complete revision of their procedure than were girls.

An opportunity to assess STAR O.3 did not arise within the natural flow of the Water Sprinkler interview, so it was omitted rather than risk distortion (Table 5.2). All the other check-points met with a high degree of success, and it seems fair to conclude that the observation skills were among the most accessible to children. Even STAR O.4 and O.5 met with success on the part of four-fifths of year six children. There are at least three reasons for this degree of success. First, observation

Table 5.2   *Observing*

Task	STAR criteria	Per cent success year six children		
		Boys $n = 58$	Girls $n = 56$	All $n = 114$
Comparison of two plastic bottles.	O.1 Notices gross features of phenomenon/object.	98	100	99
Bottle spinning under force of escaping water; spinning in reverse direction of empty bottle.	O.2 Notices details of phenomenon/object.	76	84	80
	O.3 Focuses on observations relevant to problem.	–	–	–
	O.4 Identifies (two) differences between similar objects/events.	83	80	82
	O.5 Notices (two) similarities between different objects/events.	97	97	97

is a skill which has cross-curricular value and, consequently, a lot of exposure and attention in school. Second, even when treated as a science-specific skill, it tends to be one of the first to which teachers give attention, since it is easy to plan activities for its development. Third, it is probably intrinsically less demanding than some or all of the other skills in the sense that when the demand increases, it tends to transform into measurement rather than straight observation; alternatively, the **conceptual** burden of the observation skill becomes inflated (as for example, observing structure in order to make inferences about function, as in identifying bones). Neither of the latter demands were included in the STAR observation criteria.

Children had opportunity to deploy only the first two STAR recording criteria during the task under consideration (though in the classroom setting and given more time, the same task could have been used to exploit further recording and communication skills, such as graph construction). Since only these two criteria were scored, and since they were also mutually exclusive, the results for this skill differ from those reported in other sections. For example, it is possible to infer from the data in Table 5.3 that half the sample of year six children showed no evidence of recording at all; of the 50 per cent of children who did record their results, twice as many made a continuous record during the investigation as made a summary record having completed the investigation. It seems probable that where measurements were taken, on the spot recording is likely to result in a more reliable

Table 5.3   *Recording*

Task	STAR criteria	Per cent success year six children		
		Boys $n = 58$	Girls $n = 56$	All $n = 114$
Record of outcome made at end of water sprinkler investigation.	R.1 Makes notes or drawings at end of investigation.	14	17	16
Continuous record of water sprinkler data during the investigation.	R.2 Makes notes or drawing during investigation.	34	33	37

collection and consequent interpretation of data.

Children decided for themselves whether or not they recorded, and if they did, the manner in which the record was made. In those cases in which the investigation was of a fairly cursory nature – perhaps simply confirming an impression by means of observation – recording would have offered little in the way of supporting data collection and interpretation, and this might explain why it was omitted. On the other hand, if the view is taken that the collection and discussion of evidence is of central importance to scientific activities, then the conclusion might be drawn that children should be encouraged to develop good recording habits from the outset, whatever the nature of their investigation. If the latter view is adopted, the actual levels of recording reported here might be regarded as being unacceptably low.

The performance data summarised in Table 5.4 are not specific to any particular physical property – length, volume or time – in the sense that any attempt at measuring any property enabled a child to be credited with having met the appropriate measurement criterion. By far the most commonly-used measures were of the volume of water poured into the bottle, and/or the time (duration) the bottle was spinning in either direction.

About two-thirds of children met the first measurement criterion, implying that they approached the investigation in a manner that was in some form quantified, though this did not imply the use of a standard measure.

STAR M.2 and M.3 were each met by a little over half of the sample, while only one-third were judged to have taken an adequate set of measurements of the relevant variable (e.g., timing the duration of spinning in **both** directions). STAR M.5 reveals that only 13 per cent of children checked or repeated their measurements to improve accuracy – the kind of behaviour which might be said to reflect good habits in a quantified investigation. It seems fair to suggest that there is room for improvement here; it is not always obvious to children just how to quantify a problem, but it is clear in this instance that the majority of those children who did see the value of quantifying did not see the advantage (or necessity,

Table 5.4 *Measuring*

| Task | STAR criteria | Per cent success year six children | | |
		Boys *n* = 58	Girls *n* = 56	All *n* = 114
Opportunities for counting rotations of spinning bottle; measuring volume of water poured into bottle; measuring length of string; measuring time taken for bottle to empty.	M.1 Makes comparison in terms of some quantity which is measured or estimated.	60	64	62
	M.2 Uses an appropriate unit of measurement, standard or arbitrary.	49	62	56
Might measure direction of spinning in both directions.	M.3 Chooses quantity to measure or compare such that reasonable accuracy is possible.	48	56	52
	M.4 Takes an adequate set of measurements of the relevant variable.	33	36	35
	M.5 Checks or repeats measurements to improve accuracy.	14	12	15

perhaps) of checking their measurements.

Given the closely-focused nature of the task, the high level of success with STAR P.1 should not be surprising; almost every child realised that there was some requirement to examine the spinning of the bottle (Table 5.5). Four-fifths of children interviewed in this age group indicated awareness that the length of the string would have to be changed in order to monitor its effect on the spinning of the bottle. (There was only one opportunity offered on this particular check-point.) About three-fifths of the sample could identify at least one variable to control for a fair test (STAR P.3), while two-fifths managed to identify **all** relevant variables to control. (In practice, this amounted to a requirement to identify at least two of the variables from type of thread, same bottle, constant volume of water, same size holes and identical position of holes when it was the effect of the length of the thread that was being investigated.) In the context of the Water Sprinkler task, the 'appropriate variable to measure or compare' (in effect, this had to be the duration of the spinning or the number of turns) was clearly not a very taxing demand. Eighty seven per cent of the year six sample managed to specify the dependent

Table 5.5 *Planning*

Task	STAR criteria	Per cent success year six children		
		Boys $n = 58$	Girls $n = 56$	All $n = 114$
Discussion of how investigation of spinning in two directions had been planned.	P.1 Starting point or initial actions relevant to the investigation.	97	98	97
Discussion of how an investigation into the effect of the length of the string would be conducted.	P.2 Identifies appropriate variable to change or the things to compare.	80	82	81
	P.3 Identifies at least one variable which should be kept the same for a fair test.	60	63	62
	P.4 Identifies all relevant variables to control for a fair test.	38	44	41
	P.5 Identifies an appropriate variable to measure or compare.	85	89	87

variable, when directly questioned about their proposed procedure. Other variables set in other contexts may well by found to pose a greater challenge.

Almost all children based their interpretations on the data rather than preconceived ideas (STAR I.1), but rather fewer used all the available information as the basis for their conclusions. Within the constraints of the interview, it was not possible to introduce the possibility of another set of novel data in a convincing or acceptable manner, so STAR I.3 was omitted on this occasion. The fourth Interpreting criterion proved to be the most demanding, with only about one-quarter of the sampled age-group managing to base their interpretation on the explicit number pattern in the data. STAR I.5 demanded an interpolation of a value within a series or number pattern, and revealed 44 per cent of children succeeding in meeting this criterion (Table 5.6).

The great majority of children at year six showed themselves able to mention a relevant feature (STAR H.1) or relevant concept (STAR H.2) without these components necessarily having any explanatory value. About three-quarters of the age group managed some sort of dynamic explanation in which there was an attempt to describe a mechanism. Only a quarter of responses could be described as

Table 5.6 *Interpreting*

Task	STAR criteria	Per cent success year six children		
		Boys $n = 58$	Girls $n = 56$	All $n = 114$
Interpreting the first-hand evidence of observations or measurements during the investigation.	I.1 Interpretation related to data (rather than preconceived ideas) even if only loosely.	95	91	93
Interpreting a table of data relating length of thread to number and duration of spins.	I.2 Interpretation based on all available data.	74	75	74
	I.3 Interpretation checked against new data.	–	–	–
	I.4 Interpretation explicitly based on pattern or relationship.	21	31	26
	I.5 Predication justified in terms of observed relationship.	41	47	44

conceptually accurate in a conventional scientific sense. About one-third of children were explicitly aware of the possibility of more than one explanation being an acceptable possibility.

Gender related differences in performance are not marked in Table 5.7, but on those check-points asking for hypotheses to account for the spinning of the bottle as the water escaped, boys performed significantly better than girls (check-points 35, 36 and 37, Appendix Ib). This is reflected in H.4 only.

STAR Level 4, the expression of at least one question in investigable form, is perhaps the most interesting criterion within the question raising data. Only about one-quarter of the age group reported here managed to describe a question in a form which could actually be investigated. About twice as many (60 per cent at STAR RQ.2) could suggest a question that was **potentially** investigable. About two-thirds could distinguish between questions that were investigable and those that were not when this task was presented in a focused manner. About two-fifths succeeded with STAR RQ.5, which was presented in the context of the effects of string length on spinning of the bottle; children were required to describe, in operational form, an investigation into the effect of string length on the spinning of the bottle. Necessarily, these criteria concerned with raising questions had to be presented in an explicit manner, rather than being seen to arise naturally from a line of curiosity

Table 5.7 *Hypothesizing*

Task	STAR criteria	Per cent success year six children		
		Boys $n = 58$	Girls $n = 56$	All $n = 114$
Attempting to explain: Why the bottle was spinning as the water flowed out;	H.1 Mentions relevant feature (at least) in attempting an explanation.	91	97	94
Why the bottle was spinning in the reverse direction when empty;	H.2 Gives an explanation in terms of a relevant concept (even if only by naming it).	92	91	91
What would be the effect of changing the size and portion of the holes.	H.3 Gives an explanation in terms of a mechanism involving concept (correct or incorrect).	74	73	74
	H.4 Gives explanation (mechanism) which fits evidence and is consistent with science concepts.	31	21	26
	H.5 Gives, or acknowledges, more than one explanation.	27	34	31

or enquiry. The result was probably to enhance levels of performance which, even so, would seem to leave much to be desired. While general curiosity was not in short supply, a more scientifically-framed question was encountered much less frequently.

Raising investigable questions was an area in which girls performed at levels significantly higher than boys.

THE PERFORMANCE OF INDIVIDUAL CHILDREN

Previous sections and previous chapters have examined the nature of science processes in an analytical fashion, teasing out the various components and trying to make sense of different qualities of response. It has not been the intention to suggest that the kinds of categories of behaviour described are absolutely clear cut in practice; the edges will tend to be blurred. More importantly, there is no suggestion that the various skills are likely to be seen in isolation from one another; they are

Table 5.8 *Raising questions*

Task	STAR criteria	Per cent success year six children		
		Boys $n = 58$	Girls $n = 56$	All $n = 114$
Children invited to suggest something else which could be investigated, using the same apparatus.	RQ.1 Raises more than one question (any kind).	52	57	55
	RQ.2 Raises at least one question which is potentially investigable, although the dependent variable may not be specified.	62	57	60
	RQ.3 Expresses at least one question in investigable form.	14	38	26
	RQ.4 Distinguishes, when requested, between a question which can be answered by investigation, and other types.	57	78	68
	RQ.5 Can reformulate a potentially investigable but vague question into one in which the IV and DV are identified.	38	40	39

facets of a whole, but enable the whole to be described. When process skills are used by a child conducting an investigation, the procedure is more likely to be like an organic flow of thought than a staccato assembly line of separate operations. Each phase of the activity is likely to be linked in some form of connected thought to other phases. For example, when children begin to make observations, their comments will not be limited to observational aspects of the situation alone. The process of observation will almost certainly trigger other kinds of activity within something like a sub-routine.

There is little value in taking apart the various process skills which constitute a performance, unless we can put them back together again to make sense of that performance. The following briefly-presented case histories provide some illustrations of performance as a whole. They are somewhat arbitrary in selection, in the sense that **any** child's performance is potentially fascinating to attempt to interpret;

the selections made offer some quite different approaches to performing the task. Following each description is an equally brief indication of the formative and diagnostic approach that a teacher might take in order to make sense of the child's words and actions in order to plan further appropriate experiences.

YEAR FOUR GIRL, OVERALL HIGH ACHIEVER

The children with whom she had worked made some attempt at constructing their own sprinkler, but Susan's comment was, 'There was some problems, but we did it in the end. We put two chairs back-to-back, tied string to a cane and tied the bottle on top of it. A couple of times, the bottle fell down.' Her observation of the demonstration of the spinning of the bottle as the water emptied was, 'It goes faster as it gets emptier. It makes a pattern in the water.' (This was a reference to the circular pattern that the water made as it hit the tray.) Susan's hypothesis to account for the spinning of the bottle as it emptied was, 'It's because of the weight, it weighs it down.' Her explanation of the spinning in the reverse direction offered an interesting analogy, 'It reminds me of a swing. When you wind it up, it turns round the other way. It's because its been going quite fast, it has to go back the other way.' Twisting the chains of playground swings is probably an activity familiar to many children and a small minority explained the turning of the empty bottle by reference to this experience.

Investigation

Susan filled the bottle without any indication that the amount of water which she put in was of any importance to her. She watched the emptying and spinning most attentively and commented, 'It goes faster when it's full', referring to the slowing as the bottle emptied. When the bottle was empty and had stopped spinning, she held it momentarily before releasing it and watching it turn in the other direction. When the bottle had stopped spinning in this, its empty condition, she said, 'It goes much faster when it's empty.' Her entire investigation was carried out without any measurement or counting. Every child had to make a decision as to how to interpret, 'spin as much'; in her case, the interpretation seemed to be in terms of speed. She wrote:

> The bottle spun faster when it was half full than when it was full
> When it was empty it went slower and then went faster than ever in the opposite direction.

Comment

The responses described above have the quality of being common sense rather than science-specific in nature. They demonstrate sense and intelligence without making use of the specifically scientific aspects of process skills. For example, the observation is accurate, but could go much further both in terms of specific detail and general patterns. The investigation showed an understanding of the variables involved, but was not rigorous or quantified; the question was answered to Susan's satisfaction but not in such a way that data was collected which might convince someone else. Interestingly, when specifically and directly asked about how an investigation of the effect of the length of the string could be organized, Susan responded as follows: 'Just shorten the string at different lengths; fill the bottle again for each length. Measure the water and give the bottle the same amount. Measure the string. Try and count the turns.' As it emerged, she had a clear idea of the prerequisites for a scientific investigation **in theory** but, somehow, these ideas were not sufficiently integrated into her way of doing things for her to put them into practice. It sometimes happens that children use everyday rather than scientific strategies when they perceive the **context** to be an everyday one. In this instance, the interview situation may not have been clearly identified as a **science** context.

YEAR FIVE GIRL, OVERALL HIGH ACHIEVER

Jackie indicated that she had not given the problem of constructing a seed sprinkler much thought, 'I didn't think much about it.' When asked for possible changes in her design, she suggested that it might be possible to 'Use something bigger'. Her observation was quite detailed: 'The water comes out of the holes two different ways. It turns round quite quickly then slows down and goes back the other way again.'

Investigation

Jackie's investigation was one of the longer ones encountered as the result of the fact that she decided on more than one trial, making adjustments to her procedures along the way. Initially, she filled and released the bottle and watched intently to see what happened, eventually exclaiming, 'Oh, I know!' She then poured 150 ml of water into the bottle, using a measuring cylinder, and expressed her intention to allow the bottle to spin for 60 seconds. The outcome was that her bottle had emptied before her unit of time had elapsed, and a second attempt using the same volume produced the same result. Next, she tried 250 ml for 60 seconds with no more success. Finally, she tried 500 ml and counted the number of rotations made by the bottle in a 30 second period. This worked to her satisfaction, and she went on to count the number of rotations in the reverse direction made by the empty bottle. She recorded each value immediately on completion of her measurement and on completion of her investigation, summarized her conclusions as follows:

62 68   JACKIE.

The bottle Spins more when it is emptied than
When it is full. I put 500 ml of water in and
timed it for half a minute when it was full.
and counted how many times it spun round
and timed it for half a minute
   It goes round faster when it is empty

Jackie was one of a very small minority of children who approached a measurement of the **rate** at which the bottle turned in each direction. Having thought out her plan, she was persistent in its execution despite practical set-backs. When asked about the steps she had taken to ensure a fair test, her reply was, 'Put the same amount of water in the bottle. Use the same bottle. Just let it go, instead of pushing it.'

It was interesting that the interview went on to reveal that Jackie's hypothesizing was not nearly as successful as her investigation. When asked to explain why she thought the bottle would spin as it emptied, she suggested, 'When the water comes out, it hits the tray and it turns it round. If they [the holes] were on the same side, it wouldn't go round.' In fact, there are two hypotheses here, the first one suggesting that it was the **impact** of the jet of water on the tray that caused the rotation. (This explanation was offered by a number of children, its attraction possibly residing in the fact that there is a force of impact of the water on the tray, but to explain the rotation of the bottle, this force must be conceived as working in the reverse direction. Thus, cause and effect are reversed.) Her explanation for the movement of the empty bottle was also uncertain. 'The string. I don't know why. Because of the shape of the bottle?'

Comment

This is a case of a child who was categorized as being overall a high achiever in the classroom, showing evidence of similar high achievement in science. Her particular strengths within the context of the Water Sprinkler investigation were her careful observation, her attitude of persistence and the way in which she quantified the problem. Jackie's approach could have been improved by an initial exploration of the dimensions of the task – a rough estimate of the scale of things before plunging into the investigation itself. This is clearly a child who is succeeding in school attainments, and on the basis of this interview, evidence of her willingness to reflect critically on her performance is equivocal.

She admitted that she had not given much thought to the improvement of the classroom sprinkler design. When asked whether there was anything that she might improve in the investigation that she had just conducted, she considered the question at some length before replying, 'No'. Some might take the view that a child should not be expected to offer criticisms of such a manifestly impressive investigation. Without implying in any way that a moral stance is being adopted which looks for blushing modesty in all children, it is nevertheless suggested that, almost inevitably, there is **always** some scope for improvement in a scientific investigation; there is **always** a need for caution about interpretations and an open-minded willingness to admit that the unexpected might be just around the corner.

The other trough in this particular profile of performance against STAR criteria was with hypothesizing. To be good at hypothesizing, children must have a fund of direct experiences and knowledge of secondary sources to feed their imaginations when confronted with the need to explain novel situations. They must also have the courage to 'stick out their necks' in areas of uncertainty. Children who are used to being right are often less willing to take the risk of being wrong, and this might inhibit the production of hypotheses on some occasions. In this particular case, there was a willingness to venture a guess, but the explanations were lacking in relevant conceptual background knowledge. Whether the sense of curiosity or thirst for further knowledge was lacking or remains to be developed in this particular child, is an open question. It is also a possibility that the actual subject matter about which speculation was invited was not one which captured this child's interest.

YEAR SIX BOY, OVERALL LOW ACHIEVER

Richard had already considered possibilities for the improvement of the classroom sprinkler design: 'We're thinking of joining the two bottles together and fixing the sticks, so we don't have to hold it.' Richard's observation on the demonstration release of the bottle was, 'It's twisting round. It's going faster and from side to side.' (This was a reference to a slight lateral wobble in the movement of the bottle.)

Investigation

Richard took no measurements at all but watched carefully, and then wrote the following:

```
Does the bottle spin as much after its emptied
as it did when the water was coming out?
```
The Bottle spin More Tims Thean it did wene it was full.

He had reached a clear-cut conclusion, but it took further discussion to reveal how he had come to his conclusion: 'It does it more without the water. I counted to 37 the first way. The second one, when I got to 37, I left it, because I knew it would be more. It went about ten times more.' Richard had not recorded the fact that he had actually quantified his investigation. Nor had this been obvious from direct observation of his behaviour during the interview, for he had counted mentally, not even mouthing the numbers. This is an instance in which without direct discussion and questioning, a child's performance would have been underestimated.

When it came to hypothesizing, Richard's performance could be characterized as being as good as that of any child who had been categorized as an overall high achiever. His explanation of the spinning bottle was: 'The pressure of the water is making it go round, because of the water power. There's air in the bottle as well; its pushing.' He has expressed the idea of water pressure and also seems to have the idea in some incomplete sense that there is another force, air pressure, which might have something to do with the event. His comment on the spinning of the empty bottle was: 'When the hook's going round, because there's weight on it, its going to go round the opposite way because the string's twisted.' Once again, this is a very coherent intuitive description of the phenomenon. Richard seems to take notice and try to make sense of the things which he experiences. When asked to suggest another investigation which could be carried out with the same apparatus, Richard's response was: 'Put cracks in the tray. Attach strings to a tree. All the water would fall on the seeds.' This is clearly a straight description of a course of action that does not involve a question or investigation; Richard's common-sense has led him to offer a practical solution rather than a line of enquiry.

Comment

Like many other low achieving boys, Richard rose to the occasion when offered a practical opportunity and conducted a competent investigation. However, if it had been left to Richard to reveal what he had done as a written record, his performance would have been underestimated. He needs some help to realize that recording in science must make public the thinking and data that leads to a particular interpretation, not just the conclusion alone. The mixture of upper and lower case letters in his handwriting, the elementary spelling errors and the obvious struggle with sentence structure confirm that he is having some problems with written output. These factors may have contributed to the minimal nature of his record, but, on the other hand, he has managed to convey his essential point. Although he made detailed observations, Richard left much that should have been obvious unmentioned, an outcome which might be less likely with a more confident, academically successful and loquacious child.

Another characteristic which his performance shares with many low achieving boys is the relative richness of his hypothesizing, given the opportunity to express ideas verbally. In contrast, his question raising capacity was not strong in the context of the assessment interview. It is possible that he has much to learn about just what it means to construct and conduct an investigation in the more formal scientific sense, as contrasted with his tendency to offer direct, practical solutions to problems.

From Parts to Whole in Practice

This chapter has described the performance of groups across the process skills, and also illustrated how the pieces fit together within an individual's performance. The next chapter explores some of the demands, constraints and possibilities involved in obtaining this kind of information on children's practical performance within the normal classroom setting.

6

Developing Practical Assessment
in the Classroom

Much of what has been reported in the last two chapters about the findings from the Water Sprinkler activity has relevance for the classroom by providing pointers to the likely strengths and weaknesses in children's actions and responses in practical science. But the procedures used in gathering the information can also be applied in the classroom, and it is this aspect which now becomes the focus of attention. This chapter re-examines some of the general points made in Chapter 1 against the background of the particular example of practical assessment that has been considered in detail. Its aim is to discuss the demands of assessment of science process skills in the classroom context, and to offer some support in terms of ways of making it a manageable enterprise.

The requirements of the National Curriculum Assessment, and particularly for informal, on-going assessment, are very much to the fore in this chapter. The concern is to give whatever support can be provided for teachers in relation to the assessment of pupils in terms of the Statements of Attainment for Attainment Target 1, as part of regular work. Although this does not require changes to be made in children's activities (providing these cover the parts of the Programmes of Study relating to Exploration of Science), it does require pre-planning and forward thinking on the part of the teacher if opportunities for assessment are to be taken. However, as mentioned in Chapter 1, teachers may find it necessary, at least at first, to introduce specially-devised activities which require children to use process skills and provide a more controlled opportunity for assessment. The latter part of the chapter is therefore concerned with devising more formal practical assessment.

There is more need for help in relation to science assessment for historical reasons. In English and mathematics, teachers are far more familiar with on-going diagnostic assessment than in science. A single page of a child's work may signal a battery of diagnostic information about language skills. For example, the range and richness of vocabulary, the imagery and expressiveness, sentence construction, perhaps phonetic spelling, the perceptual-motor control in the hand-writing, reversals in letters or words: all of these may be taken in almost at a glance. Most teachers make these sorts of diagnostic judgements daily with barely a second thought, in relation to children's work in language and mathematics. In primary science, the expertise of teachers and the means for making more comprehensive assessments 'on the hoof' in the classroom pose more novel demands, and widespread confidence remains to be firmly established.

ON-GOING ASSESSMENT OF SCIENCE PROCESS SKILLS

As in any activity, good technique in assessment will give more time, not only in the sense of managing available time effectively, but in focusing on the essential points and allowing the irrelevant to be ignored. This reduces enormously the information load and the stress that may accompany it. A coherent framework for viewing children's behaviour will enable it to be looked at selectively, almost as though the actions are occurring in slow motion. Technique gives the teacher time, just as technique in sports gives the player time, for example, to face fast bowling in cricket or a first service in tennis.

Four ways in which technique can be developed to meet assessment responsibilities will be discussed:

(1) building up the expertise of **knowing what to expect** when practical investigations are on the agenda;
(2) considering what has to be done **'on the spot' and what can be left for later consideration** in a less pressured moment;
(3) **making the most of opportunities for assessment;**
(4) blurring the distinctions between **teaching, learning and assessment.**

KNOWING WHAT TO EXPECT

The example of 'at a glance' assessment referred to above reflects the position of an experienced teacher who carries a knowledge of progression in the language curriculum in his or her head. Such knowledge is not learned and memorized point by point. Nor is it acquired overnight. It is accumulated through experience of children and a firm notion of what language development involves. It becomes such a fundamental and coherent way of looking at a child's performance as to seem self-evident. In fact, it is far from self-evident as any attempt to help a novice to acquire the same skills will very soon reveal.

In the assessment of science process skills as revealed in children's practical classroom investigations, the proportion of teachers who would claim to carry a coherent mental vision of the science curriculum in their heads is probably a minority. There will no doubt be a fairly long gestation period during which the science curriculum will more likely be physically located close at hand rather than in the head. If the science curriculum is to be comprehended and internalized by teachers, it will have to make sense as a coherent whole such that teachers develop the 'feel' of the whole thing in terms of the important landmarks which children reach and the inter-relatedness of these. In earlier chapters, we have endeavoured to specify and exemplify the range of process skills and the behaviours associated with each. They have been identified and considered as separable skills being used in the context of a whole investigation. In practice, these skills are not likely to be used separately, but are seen in recurring clusters and patterns, so that it is possible to anticipate which ones will be in evidence at particular points in an investigation. It should, therefore, be possible to use this information to make the process of gathering information about performance more controlled and manageable. This can be illustrated by some examples of activities and the behaviours which might arise in association with them.

Children might, following some field work, be **observing** the behaviour of snails kept temporarily in a transparent tank, or earthworms in a wormery. The undulating muscular ripple associated with a snail's movement becomes apparent as it moves across a transparent surface, as does the slime trail that it lays down. The changing body configuration of the earthworm can be equally compelling viewing. Observations which intrigue do so because they stimulate curiosity, and curiosity is very close to enquiry. Consequently, children almost inevitably begin to move from observational descriptions to **hypothesizing** about reasons for what they see. At the same time, observation leads to questions being posed, some of which will be in investigable form, such as, 'how do they find their food, by smell or sight?' In a group, there are likely to be different points of view; with some experience, children are able to suggest investigations which will help to test hypotheses, answer questions and perhaps resolve differences of opinion. If the children are not yet at the point at which they automatically raise questions or express hypotheses in investigable form, an input from the teacher – 'How could you test that idea?' 'What would you need to do to find that out?', for example – may spur them into doing so.

It is also likely that the idea of quantifying observations will arise in response to the questions they raise, e.g., 'How much longer is the worm when it's stretched out than when it's small?'; or (much more difficult because it entails the measurement of rate, the ratio between distance travelled and time), 'How fast does a snail

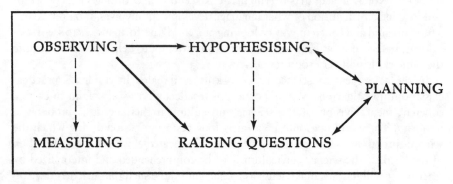

Figure 6.1   *'Start up' skills cluster.*

move?'. Figure 6.1 summarizes the cluster of skills that a teacher might expect to see in this sub-routine, developing from a 'starting up' activity.

Once children have defined their general area of interest in the form of a question or hypothesis, their enquiry has to be transformed into a plan of action: something that can be put into operation. This takes them into the **planning** phase of activity during which they will be making decisions about manipulating variables. They will have to consider which variable they intend to investigate by changing it (the independent variable) while all other variables are controlled (kept the same); which variable will be **measured** (the dependent variable) and what apparatus and instruments are required to carry out such measurements. (They will not always decide to measure the dependent variable; often, it will be decided that **observation** alone is sufficient.) It is possible that there will also be **critical reflection** centred on the planning at this point, perhaps stimulated by the group, or promoted by a question from the teacher, 'Will that tell you what you want to know? Can you think of another way of . . .'

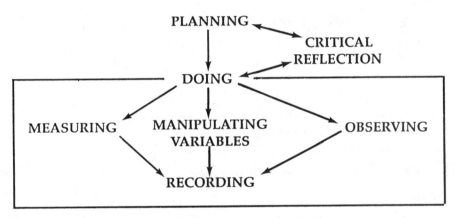

Figure 6.2   *'Planning and doing' skills cluster.*

The planning phase is not usually protracted, especially for young children and those less familiar with conducting their own investigations. They will be eager to launch into the action to see what happens since they lack the experience to anticipate actions (see Chapter 2, page 25). One might expect the activity to correspond to the planning, but in practice this is quite often not the case and, indeed, the action might be rather minimal if it did. Plans seldom mention all that needs to be done and so cannot be taken as indicating what an investigation will be in practice. Thus the 'doing', involving the physical manipulation of variables and the making of **observations** and possibly of **measurements**, is quite distinct from the planning. **Recording** of the observations or data takes place during or after the doing. Figure 6.2 summarizes the 'planning and doing' cluster of skills.

Having collected the data – about wriggling worms, sliding snails, spinning bottles or whatever – conclusions have to be drawn. Essentially, this means **interpreting** the data that has been **recorded** in relation to the question that has been

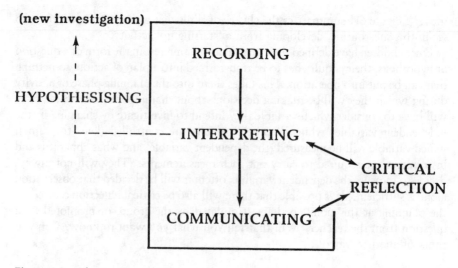

Figure 6.3   *The 'interpreting' cluster of process skills.*

┌─── OBSERVING ───┐

1a   observe familiar materials and events in their immediate
      environment, at first hand, using their senses.   ☐

─ ─

2b   identify simple differences, such as *hot / cold, rough / smooth*.   ☐

─ ─

3b   identify and describe simple variables that change over time, *such
      as growth of a plant.*   ☐

─ ─

3d   select and use simple instruments to enhance observations, for
      example, *a stop clock or hand lens.*   ☐

└───┘

┌─── RAISING QUESTIONS ─────────────────────────────────────┐

2a   ask questions and suggest ideas of the 'how', 'why' and 'what
      will happen if' variety.   ☐

└───┘

┌─── HYPOTHESISING ───┐

3a   formulate hypotheses ('*this ball will bounce higher . . .*').   ☐

PLANNING

3c distinguish between a 'fair' and an 'unfair' test. □

MEASURING

2c use non-standard and standard measures (*hand spans; rulers*). □

3e quantify variables, as appropriate, to the nearest labelled division of simple measuring instruments, e.g. *a rule*. □

RECORDING

2d list and collate observations. □

2f record findings in charts, drawings, other appropriate forms. □

3f record experimental findings, e.g., *in tables and bar charts*. □

3g interpret simple pictograms. □

INTERPRETING

2e interpret findings by associating one factor with another (*pupils' perceptions – 'light objects float', 'thin wood is bendy'*). □

3h interpret observations in terms of a generalised statement, e.g., *the greater the suspended weight, the longer the spring*. □

COMMUNICATING

1b describe and communicate their observations, ideally through talking in groups or by other means, within their class. □

3i describe activities carried out by sequencing the major features. □

Figure 6.4 *Sequenced checklist of AT1 criteria for KS1.*

posed. This is likely to occur within the small group which conducted the investigation before being **communicated** to the class as a whole. Typically, there will be some **critical reflection** as to why things were conducted as they were. Equally likely, the data will give rise to alternative **hypotheses**, and the whole cycle of investigation will move into action again. The 'interpreting' cluster of skills is summarized in Figure 6.3.

This method of grouping the process skills is a way of making sense of a rapid and unbroken flow of activity. In thinking of the skills as occurring in probable sequences, clusters or cycles, a complex whole is broken down into sub-routines which have some logical relationship to one another. Teachers who have this kind of coherent view of the inter-relationships between the science processes (and it need not be identical to that that is outlined above), find it relatively easy to approach a group at work and quickly focus on the particular process skills which are being deployed or discussed. This helps to avoid information overload.

Taking this line of thinking a stage further, it is possible to reassemble all the Statements of Attainment of AT1 in a sequence which reflects the unfolding phases of an investigation, and to use such a summary as a recording checklist. The STAR teachers did just this, using an instrument that included all the statements for levels 1 to 5 (see Appendix 3). Odd criteria, such as references to safety, have to be fitted in wherever seems appropriate – in the example shown, safety is considered as part of the 'planning and doing' phase. A similar checklist for levels 1 to 3 only is shown in Figure 6.4.

'ON-THE-SPOT' AND DEFERRED ASSESSMENT

There are seventeen AT1 criteria to be considered at Key Stage 1 (Levels 1 to 3) and a further fourteen to be considered in the years up to the end of year six. Not all these criteria apply at all points and not all children have to be assessed at once so if this were all the assessment which had to be done, it would present little problem in a class where children were regularly involved in practical investigative work. However, there are other things to be assessed and other parts of the curriculum to attend to.

Practical science presents two particular difficulties for assessment. The first problem is that children are producing evidence of their skills and abilities almost incessantly and simultaneously one with another. Although teachers would not wish it otherwise (assuming that whole-class, one hand up at a time, 'speak-when-spoken-to' teaching is not the prevailing method), a 'hive' of activity is not the easiest environment in which to monitor significant behaviours of individual participants.

The second problem is that many telling signs are ephemeral, or as Keats put it, 'writ in water'. A fleeting manipulation of apparatus may reveal hidden depths of understanding; a few spoken words might convey an unexpected comprehension of an idea; perhaps doing something or even doing nothing at a particular moment (e.g. **not** attempting to take an instantaneous temperature reading, which would actually be inaccurate), will demonstrate an insight. All of these outcomes –

gestures, actions, spoken words – may be valid forms of evidence of skills, knowledge and understanding. For assessment purposes, unless the teacher is on the spot with focused attention, the evidence might as well not have existed.

Assessment needs evidence, a trace, a warm trail; evidence needs to be collected, and it must have a witness to connect it to events. (Talk of 'evidence' perhaps seems legalistic, but it is used in the sense of trying to be fair and objective, to avoid personal prejudice and inconsistency in public judgements about children's performance.)

Conscious of the impossibility of seeing and noting every event in the classroom which might be capable of providing insight into each child's performance, some teachers have resorted to electronic extensions to their senses, in the form of tape recorders and video cameras. A group of children might be started on an activity and the tape left running, to be analysed at some later time. This is an example of deferred assessment, since although the evidence is **collected** on the spot, decisions about its **interpretation** are made later.

Although intended to be time saving, recordings of this kind may turn out to be more of a burden on time than anticipated. Recordings have enormous value as a means of sharing examples of actions and outcomes, illustrations of how different children may be seen to meet various criteria. But this purpose is quite different from the purposes of deferred assessment, which is to reduce the burden on 'here-and-now' demands on the teacher, while simultaneously trying to avoid missing assessment opportunities which may occur only infrequently. For this purpose, the considerable play-back time required tends to counterbalance the value of the information obtained.

Fortunately, there are a number of ways in which children can learn to leave a trace of their activity which can be subjected to the teacher's scrutiny at a later moment. The most obvious product may be a drawing, a diagram, a piece of writing or a combination of these. Although our concern here is with the outcomes of practical activities, there is no reason to exclude the possibility of pencil and paper methods for summarizing the outcomes of practical sessions. The use of paper and pencil assessment of process skills is the subject of an associated volume (Schilling *et al.*, 1990); here we restrict consideration to work carried out in the process of, or as a result of, practical investigation.

The recording used by young children very often incorporates the products of their investigations – cut-outs of shadows, routes of slime trails of snails, models or constructions, paint tracks of cars rolling down ramps, etc. (Figure 6.5) These are effective because they are direct and concrete, connecting the product directly to the process of the activity. They are also convenient in providing the teacher with a relatively durable record of events for later consideration, which might include a discussion of the method used, the fairness of the procedures, children's ideas about measurement possibilities, and so on.

In cases in which the writing, drawing or construction is sufficiently unambiguous, it may be possible for a teacher to carry out the assessment not just after the event of the investigation, but also, in the absence of the child. In other cases, it will be necessary for judgements about performance made after the event

Figure 6.5   *Children's record of car journeys down a ramp.*

to be in the presence of the child, when the written record is used as the basis for discussion between teacher and child, certain aspects being probed and clarified by the teacher's questioning. The responses to 'Tell me more about how you did this . . .' or 'Which of these did you do first?' or 'How did you measure this?' elicit information about details which may not have been recorded, but which help the teacher to judge the nature of the practical activity. Without such discussions, it is very difficult to gain any clear impression of children's critical reflection, for example.

Not every skill can be assessed by means of a record or product, whether or not the child is present. For example, the way children use measuring instruments in the context of their investigations may be quite different to the way they perform 'on demand'. There is often a difference between having knowledge of procedures and knowing how to apply that knowledge usefully, to meet a need. For example, whereas most children could demonstrate how a stopclock is used to measure time, far fewer used it accurately or appropriately in the Water Sprinkler investigation. The best indication of their measurement skill was obtained by direct, on-the-spot observation.

MAKING THE MOST OF OPPORTUNITIES FOR ASSESSMENT

There has been considerable debate, in the context of the nature and form of the external assessments (the Standard Assessment Tasks) about the extent to which more than one criterion at a time can be reliably applied. The reliability here is essentially that of the teacher's judgement in deciding whether or not a child's output matches the requirements of a given criterion. One line of thought is to say that the teacher should be focusing on one aspect of the performance, with one criterion in mind. Even though the activity seems to provide opportunity for other skills or understanding to be assessed, the limited focus is maintained. The assessment judgement to be made by the teacher is thus limited to a single on/off type of decision as to whether or not that single criterion has been met in the child's performance. The limitation applies to other criteria at a particular level and to criteria at different levels relating to the same skill or understanding. In the case of a SAT, this means that component tasks are devised to assess criteria at different levels; a child attempts the tasks at the level at which the teacher considers he or she is likely to succeed. This is called 'differentiation by task' and is also known as 'tailored testing', because the assessment item is matched to the individual child. In the case of whole investigations, it is the case that several assessments are made, covering a range of the criteria at a particular level for AT1. However, a specified question is asked (or sub-task provided) for each Statement.

A quite different way of proceeding is to offer the child a more open-ended invitation to show what he or she can do within an activity which has the potential to elicit performance which might be at one of two or more different levels ('levels' in National Curriculum terms). Whereas tailored testing throws only one ball in the air to be caught or dropped, in 'differentiation by outcome' we are unsure of what we might have to catch. Judgements have to be made between the two or three relevant criteria which children's responses might match.

The Water Sprinkler activity is designed for differentiation by outcome. The benefits of this approach are that the overall assessment process may be much more economical; the potential hazard is that with more criteria to bear in mind, reliability of judgement might be thought to be compromised. However, as familiarity with the Statements increases – as it is bound to do in time – and, hopefully, some of the rough edges which make the statements difficult to use will be smoothed as a result of feedback from use, this disadvantage will decrease.

Thinking in terms of teachers' assessment, it seems most improbable that classroom practice will favour anything other than differentiation by outcome as the most usual mode of activity. An element of open-endedness is essential to practical investigations and it would be ridiculous to ignore levels of achievement that are higher than anticipated, simply because they are not currently on the teacher's assessment agenda. At the same time, the precision of the information required for assessment of a particular Statement of Attainment will have to be recognized. Within an investigation where assessment is to be made, teachers will need to ensure that there is opportunity for the specific aspects of performance to be revealed if they are present, and avoid being influenced by related but not specific evidence. Moreover, they will continue to adjust the demand of an activity to the level a child can meet, thus combining elements of task and outcome differentiation in classroom assessment.

With experience, too, teachers are also likely to find and exploit situations which enable both science skills and other achievements to be assessed in the course of cross-curricular activities. Increased familiarity with the curricula will enhance the possibilities of this kind of opportunistic assessment.

TEACHING, LEARNING AND ASSESSMENT

The assessment activities described in this book have little in common with some traditional testing scenarios. For example, there is no assumption of a need for a hushed, expectant and tense atmosphere. It was gratifying to confirm that children enjoyed participation in the Water Sprinkler investigation, but this was by design, not accident. Enjoyment was probably because they were able to manipulate materials freely, were given control of the activity, found the outcomes to be intrinsically interesting and, perhaps most important of all, left with a sense of success. Most children are likely to enjoy the exploration of the properties of water that the Water Sprinkler task made available. To increase the level of anxiety by conducting the assessment in an atmosphere of judgemental silence would offer no advantage and would probably be found to be an inhibiting and counter-productive atmosphere by most children. If we wish to see what children are optimally capable of doing, it seems a reasonable requirement that a conducive atmosphere in which to do so should be generated. Assessment of the science curriculum should be designed to sample classroom behaviours, in the sense of looking at a small selection of representative examples of the kind of things to which children have been exposed in the classroom. There is no justification for an assessment environment which is even mildly hostile or alien (unless the purpose is to assess reactions to stressful conditions, an irrelevance to primary education).

Since the notion of user-friendly assessment may be opposite to many peoples' personal experience of having been at the receiving end of examinations, the relationship between learning and assessment will be explored a little further at this point. There are some fundamental implications for the teacher's role in the way that this relationship is treated, for it will be argued that many, probably most, assessment decisions can be centred on or derived from normal classroom situations.

Curriculum or 'learning' materials and assessment activities may share many features in common. In either case, stimulus material is provided which should secure a child's involvement and encourage a response of some kind. The main difference between the two is that the curriculum activity introduces what is predominantly a **learning** opportunity, the assessment activity introduces a **performance** opportunity, an invitation for the child to show what he or she can do. In the latter case, there is more emphasis on gaining feedback about a child's progression. It might be expected that learning and assessment activities must also differ in the degree of novelty which they introduce, but if the assessment is of **understanding** rather than **recall**, while the task might be familiar, the context in which it is set need not be. To be 'fair', a test does not have to be based on material which has been 'learnt' or seen before. Indeed, to assess understanding, a novel setting will help to avoid the possibility of children using direct recall rather than the **application** of knowledge.

Another respect in which learning and assessment materials of good quality may be similar, is that both are capable of offering children the opportunity to experience **success**, at their own level. This implies that the behaviour and the range of possible outcomes should not be so narrow as to convey the message to children that, in a test, there is only success or failure, in the manner of jumping through hoops. Whatever the differences between children in level or rate of progress, good practice in teaching, with any age group and with any achievement level, always strives to enhance children's own sense of competence. Good assessment practice can rest on the same assumptions: bad assessment practice assesses children's failures; good assessment assesses children's successes. In either climate, children are undoubtedly sensitive to the prevailing ethos, and the implicit messages associated with each contribute to their self-perceptions.

Given the similarities discussed above, the introduction of assessment opportunities as a normal and integrated component of classroom activity need not be an intrusive strategy, and the possibilities for using teachers' time efficiently and economically should be apparent. Planning is the key to preventing assessment from controlling the curriculum and dominating teachers' time. Assessment opportunities may be present in children's activities but not seized unless the best way to do this has been thought out. It is useful to recognize the different kinds of evidence that are required for different types of performance to be assessed and the frequency or infrequency of opportunities for assessment. Clearly, infrequently occurring opportunities have to take precedence over those aspects which can be assessed on other occasions.

Evidently, some areas of the core curriculum will be more frequently visited than others. For example, the production of written products of some kind is likely to be a daily component of the language curriculum. Other outcomes relating to areas within the Programmes of Study may occur sufficiently infrequently that teachers will want to make special efforts in order to be on the spot, recording device poised, when they occur. Finally, there will be outcomes which it will only be possible to witness by setting up situations to ensure their occurrence, either because they constitute rarely visited curricular backwaters, or because gaps are found in individual children's records because of absences or need for special help.

Having decided what **could** be assessed, the teacher has to decide what **will** be assessed on a particular occasion and plan the activity so that the information will be gathered. This may mean ensuring that children produce something, or that the teacher is able to observe what is done at a particular point or engages the children in discussion. The more a teacher manages to integrate assessment into the normal teaching/learning classroom routine, the more useful and the less burdensome and time-consuming it is likely to be.

MORE FORMAL PRACTICAL ASSESSMENT

In addition to the reasons suggested earlier for using activities specially devised for checking on children's progress, there will be times when teachers will need activities which will provide performance benchmarks for children in a class or in several classes in a school. Such activities are likely to be based on normal science investigations in school. This origin will ensure that they are feasible, that they are realistic for children to undertake and make reasonable demands on teachers (for example, only require the teacher to be in one place at any one time and monitoring only one outcome at a time). A good assessment activity has to be imaginative as well as comprehensive, and there is no precise formula for developing one from likely practical activities. However, it is possible to list some considerations which should help teachers to avoid some of the potential frustrations and difficulties involved.

First, we will consider the development of practical assessment procedures in terms of:

• practical classroom considerations;
• the setting and the subject matter;
• the coverage of the process skills;
• the teacher as a variable in the assessment process.

Finally, we look again at the whole purpose of practical work, which formative and diagnostic assessment is intended to further, and particularly at the role of social skills in practical investigations.

PRACTICAL CLASSROOM CONSIDERATIONS

Safety must be a first consideration in any practical activity since there will inevitably be times when the teacher's attention is elsewhere. Avoid the use of mains electricity. Prohibit the smelling or tasting of any liquids other than under direct teacher supervision; this will establish good habits in preparation for the time when children encounter potentially dangerous, odourless and colourless liquids which cannot be assumed to be water. Avoid any objects or equipment going into children's mouths and then being passed around – if blowing through objects is required, sterilize them or use disposable items. Avoid the opportunity for children to put small objects in their ears or nostrils. Avoid glassware and sharp objects; use plastic where possible.

Resources should be simple, cheap and readily obtainable, otherwise their consumption and replacement will be a source of anxiety to the teacher and an inhibition to the children. It is a myth that science requires special, expensive equipment; primary school children do not need particle accelerators. Darwin spent most of his life investigating the activities of earthworms in his garden and revolutionized scientific thinking about soil. Sound, light and shadows, air and water are all virtually free, and excellent raw materials for investigations. For materials such as wood, plastic, paper, cardboard, etc., it is often possible to locate sources of factory offcuts, though in quantities which may necessitate sharing between schools.

Scale is important to children in the primary age range. Something has to happen in an investigation; something changes while other things are kept constant. It is critical to children that the change is large enough and obvious enough to be observed or handled easily. This is particularly so when the practical investigation is carried out as a group activity. The scale of time is also important; if an event is the focus of attention, there should be no danger of missing it in a blink, nor of children becoming bored and distracted by events which are barely perceptible and take an age to happen. Most children love practical activities and their interest and engagement need to be sustained by ensuring clear events and outcomes within the task.

From a teacher's point of view, a science activity which takes place in a classroom must not be invasive in terms of space or its likelihood of distracting children engaged in other activities.

Maintenance needs will be an important consideration for teachers. The materials and procedures must be sufficiently robust to perform reliably without constant repair or attention; it is also desirable that the set-up should be useable by several groups of children in turn. If key materials are consumed during an investigation, they must be quickly and easily replaceable. The point of having a standardized procedure is that it can be easily replicated with different groups of children without the expenditure of too much time in setting up and maintenance.

If the activity is as far as possible self-evident to children, it can be pupil directed, thus making minimal demands on direct teacher oversight. This allows the teacher the option of engaging in other activities until such time as an activity requiring on-the-spot monitoring occurs.

Ethical considerations are important when investigations involve living animals. That children will demonstrate care and consideration for animals should not be assumed; this is something that many children must be exposed to at school, under teacher supervision. Even 'observation' of animals can be intrusive and damaging, usually quite unwittingly.

THE SETTING AND THE SUBJECT MATTER

Children's interest must be engaged if there is to be any likelihood of gaining an indication of how competent they are in performing investigations. If the practical assessment activity has grown out of science topic work, teachers will be aware of the factors which make the activity enjoyable and appealing. In assessment, there is usually less time available for setting the scene than in more routine classroom projects. For this reason, it helps if the practical assessment is capable of making an immediate impact on children, stimulating their interest fairly immediately. If children do not feel motivated, performance is likely to be depressed and the assessment will have little validity.

The content of an activity, for children, means 'what this is all about'. It is at this very global level that children tend to make judgements about their competence in relation to the task. The same is true of adults, many of whom are likely to say 'I know nothing about . . .' followed by their particular blind spots. Although knowledge as such may not be needed, and indeed they may know more about the subject than they suppose, this perception of the subject being alien inhibits willingness to become involved. Familiar and 'friendly' settings will help to avoid such reactions. Very impersonal settings of an abstract nature will be the most off-putting. Problems are sometimes set in a way which suggests very little context at all; they rely on an intrinsic motivation towards solving problems. Many children, girls in particular, are not in the least motivated by such problems; they are left 'cold' if there is no apparent reason, purpose or meaningful outcome to the activity.

There can be a very wide range of content or subject matter for practical investigations, since the main focus is on the science processes rather than science concepts. However, the subject matter must be essentially 'scientific', meaning that it is something which relates to the physical world and where the use of process skills can lead to increased understanding. The National Curriculum, specifying as it does the knowledge and understanding which children are required to have, is the obvious lead to suitable topic areas. However, it is certainly the case that some Attainment Targets lend themselves to investigations more easily than others. For example, investigations centred on sound or light can be readily constructed, while this is not so for 'The Earth in Space' where learning and assessment is more easily approached through secondary sources such as books, posters and films. As noted in Chapter 1 the subject matter also has an important bearing on the performance of an investigation. If we know something about a particular subject – how a pendulum, sound production or light transmission 'works', we will have a better idea of what it is relevant to quantify and measure, what needs to be kept the same to make our test fair, and so on. In other words, children's science knowledge will have an impact on the effectiveness of their use of science processes. The children's existing knowledge must therefore be considered in deciding the content. Familiarity is a good thing as long as the question under investigation is not one where the result can be recalled or worked out from previous experience.

Gender differences are a well-established fact of children's scientific perfor-mance, and these may be associated with the different kinds of subject matter presented. For example, it has been found that girls are likely to perform better than boys when the content concerns plants and animals (provided the animals are furry, not creepie-crawlies). Boys tend to perform better than girls when the content is of a physical science nature, especially when this is de-personalized, as with rollers on ramps, loads on bridges and such-like. Provided teachers are aware of such factors, we can avoid unwittingly penalizing one group or the other.

COVERAGE OF PROCESS SKILLS

Different kinds of statements. While the effort is being made to create special assessment activities, it is worthwhile ensuring that all the Statements of Attainment for Attainment Target 1 are covered. The statements fall into three kinds:

- certain 'core' statements which would naturally be included in any practical activity (relating to observation, communication, raising questions, 'fair' testing);
- statements which would be included only where measurement is involved in finding how one variable changes with another (quantifying variables, interpreting observations, recording in tables, bar charts and graphs);

- statements which do not naturally fall into an investigation but can be assessed within the same context by adding on specific questions (interpreting pictograms and bar charts, follow written instructions).

Matching the range of statements to pupils. Clearly, the sophistication of a practical investigation has to match the achievement level of the children. It would be pointless, and quite destructive, to face KS 1 children with investigations which extend to Level 5. Similarly, year six children must be given greater challenges than those in year three. Here we are revisiting the issue of 'tailoring' or differentiation by task or outcome and, not unexpectedly, we find that a compromise is the best solution. We require tasks that cover a small range only of National Curriculum levels, so that these can be validly assessed. Children at the ends of the achievement distribution in a class may be given different versions to suit their likely success.

Making different versions of an investigation is an economic way of using resources and avoids some children feeling that they have been left out of something which others have done. For example, an investigation concerning the size of drops of water that fall from a small dropper can be framed in different ways, such as the following:

- **Levels 1 and 2** Using plastic pipette droppers, children make drops on non-absorbent paper. They are asked to make single drops by squeezing the pipette as little as possible to make the drop fall. Are all the drops the same size? What happens to the size if the dropper is held at different heights above the paper? The children are asked to record their findings in some way (e.g., by drawing round the drops and noting the height beside each one).

- **Levels 2, 3 and 4** Using plastic droppers with a range of nozzle sizes (easily arranged by cutting the ends at different points) children are asked to make single drops and to examine their sizes. The question is posed as to whether the size of the nozzle makes any difference. Clear, plastic sheeting and squared paper, as well as rulers and handlenses, are provided. Also, the children are told that they can use any other equipment if they wish. They are asked to record their work individually on a sheet which has space for a written record, for a table of results and for an interpretation ('what I found . . .'). In discussion, children are asked what else might be affecting the size and what other things they could investigate about the drops. They are shown a bar chart of drop sizes from the same sized hole of thick oil, honey, shampoo, water and petrol and questioned about which is the largest and smallest and whether they could account for the differences.

- **Levels 4 and 5** The children are given equipment consisting of droppers of different sizes, small measuring cylinders and various surfaces for dropping the water on to. They are asked to practise making single drops and then to think about what might make a difference to the size of the drop. They are asked to consider how they will measure 'size' of drop, by area or by the amount of water in the drop. They should plan to investigate a possible cause of variation in size, carrying out their tests as carefully as possible. They are told that they can use any other equipment they wish if it is available.

While the activity may look essentially the same, it clearly makes different demands on the pupils. In particular, the rough notion of size of drop as being the area over which it spreads is accepted in the first two versions, but is challenged in the third. This will bring in a whole new range of measurement skills and, of course, the conceptual understanding of volume. The greater conceptual base required for investigation at Level 5 is indicated in the statement: 'Use concepts, knowledge and skills to suggest simple questions and design investigations to answer them'.

This 'water drop' example is intended to give some indication of how normal classroom activities can be used as a basis of more formal practical assessment when there is need for this. It may also indicate how assessment opportunities can be planned into investigations that are a regular part of work.

THE TEACHER AS A VARIABLE IN THE ASSESSMENT PROCESS

However objective we try to be in matching children's performance to criteria, there is always the possibility of variation between the judgements of teachers. This may be the result of slightly differing interpretations of the criteria, different past experiences of what children have achieved, or different expectations of what children might be expected to achieve. Personalities of teachers and children may also interact in particular ways which colour perceptions of performance. It is desirable, at least, to develop a sensitivity to such possibilities.

It happens frequently that teaching becomes an activity which isolates individuals professionally, within their own classrooms. While it is relatively easy to **talk** in the staffroom about common experiences, it is more difficult to share those experiences in a more direct manner. Team teaching offers scope for such exchanges of perceptions. The STAR project provided supply teacher cover to enable teachers to work together with a single class of children (see Chapter 1, page 10). In the context of these opportunities for systematic observation in a colleague's class, it was a revelation for many teachers to share their classroom, either to observe and offer feedback, or to be observed. Initial feelings of apprehension are understandable, but are soon overcome when the value to everyday practice of the resulting discussions becomes apparent. Such an arrangement might be difficult for most teachers to experience, but there are other ways of organizing interchanges which produce approximately the same outcomes.

One possibility is to use audio or video recordings of classroom interactions, and to replay these while subjecting their contents to analysis within a group discussion. Some schools have organized professional development sessions which take recordings of children's classroom behaviours and scrutinize these, trying to reach consensus on interpreting the recorded behaviour in terms of assessment criteria. In the sense that a recording permits any number of action replays of ambiguous or controversial points, there are advantages over direct observation. Even though not all details may be clearly recorded, the important function is to clarify the meaning of a particular criterion and agree what information is sought as the basis for decision making.

In all essential respects, such a discussion is a moderation meeting, for it seeks to establish a mode or common understanding and usage of the criteria which diverse individuals are attempting to apply as common standards. Moderation should not be thought of as a process of bending the knee to a clear-sighted and dispassionate outside authority. It must involve the recognition that teachers become passionately involved in thinking about the progress of the children they teach. There are different ways of interpreting the same behaviour, and group discussions should attempt to reach an unambiguous working definition, preferably with consensus. In this way, the impact of individual teachers as variables in the assessment process may be minimized without implying that it can ever be totally eliminated.

INTELLECTUAL DEVELOPMENT, SOCIAL SKILLS AND PRACTICAL INVESTIGATIONS

For primary children particularly, practical investigation has a central role in learning science. It consists essentially of children answering questions by direct interaction with the world around them. This does more than provide them with the answers to their questions; it gives them control of their own learning, a realization of how questions are answered (not from books, but in the beginning from actions on things), and the start of an appreciation of the nature of science. But practical work is not an adequate phrase for this activity since it excludes the social side of the learning opportunities which it makes possible.

Investigation involves mental as well as physical activity, and communication is an important element. Exchanges of views and ideas with others often leads to an understanding emerging which is truly the result of combined thinking and which advances the development of all involved. However, to arrive at the position where children can genuinely share the same practical experiences and indulge in a co-operative exchange of views requires a set of circumstances and a skill on the part of the teacher which are certainly not universal. In particular, there has to be a certain social climate for practical work which it takes time to establish.

Many of the teachers participating in the STAR project were pioneers in developing activities and techniques for which there was little precedent within their schools. Over the three years of the project, most of these teachers took on a new class each year, usually a different year group. As a consequence, it was not always possible to build on the progress in skills, routines and expectations that had been made with the previous group. These group differences were also very noticeable during the classroom observation sessions when the STAR teachers worked with colleagues in other classrooms. It became evident that children, both individually and as a group, were at different points in development from class to class in terms of the social skills needed for practical work to run in a smooth, orderly and constructive fashion. Each new group to which practical science was introduced needed a gradual induction to the methods and organization; to attempt to implement change too quickly may easily result in children becoming overloaded and confused.

When teachers encounter the unavoidable problems associated with attempting to implement practical activities for the first time, there may be some temptation to attribute the failure to shortcomings in the children: 'You can't do that sort of activity with children in our school; things get broken or go missing; they don't know how to share.' It may well be true that children lack the necessary skills; if they do, they have to learn them. It is worth looking in some detail at what these skills are in the expectation that it may be possible to apply a checklist to the social behaviours which enable practical science to be a success. By looking at practical sessions analytically, we can identify the component social skills. This makes the job of fostering development less awesome, because we can approach the task of identifying and modifying the necessary social behaviours in progressive steps, rather than trying to implement a range of changes all at once.

Many teachers of younger children start with children all having the same materials and equipment, each participating in the observation, manipulation or whatever else is required on an individual basis, but in unison with the whole class. There are obvious disadvantages to persisting with this mode of involvement. The demands on equipment dictate that only the simplest materials can be made available; the procedures, also, have to be within the capabilities of every participant. Gradually, children can be introduced to the greater autonomy which small group work offers. This also allows the teacher to operate a more flexible science timetable, with groups working on different topics. In attempting to shift to this mode of operating, the major areas of concern (and some of these are very mundane) are likely to be the following:

Apparatus and equipment distribution – are children able to decide their own needs and collect materials in a safe and orderly fashion?

The eventual aim will be to encourage children to decide their own needs and collect materials accordingly. Initially, the novelty may be too much for children to cope with and fetching materials can degenerate into a competitive scramble. In the early stages, it might be necessary for the teacher to distribute the materials to each group, or allocate responsibility to one child within each group, gradually moving to giving the children more autonomy. Good resource organization will make it easier for children to cope. Teachers lives are made easier if equipment is easily accessible rather than locked away. Children need to feel familiar with the materials they may choose to use.

Clearing away and cleaning up – can children see what is needed and organize it themselves?

Ten per cent of allocated science time spent on clearing up was not unusual in observed sessions during the STAR project; on occasions it was more than this. The more children are able to manage themselves, the more time is freed for the more rich and exciting aspects of science; good habits in maintaining a clean and uncluttered working area should be developed at an early stage, as much as anything out of considerations for safety.

Rotating roles in a group – are children able to organize themselves so that everyone feels that they have had an equal opportunity to participate?

Some individuals may have acquired greater status than others in a group; children vary in their sensitivity to the needs of others. Some STAR teachers allocated roles to children initially, to ensure that all tasks (including the less glamorous recording role) were covered, and that all children had an opportunity to participate in all aspects of practical work at some time. With this support, children should gradually take over the responsibility for the sharing of roles for themselves.

Expressing a point of view – is each child able to make a verbal contribution to support the functioning of the group?

Practical activities are based in 'doing', but if they are not also about thinking, they achieve little that is significant. In a group situation, it is important for children to recognize that everyone's contribution must be heeded, and that there is almost an obligation to make a contribution. Scientific thinking is about the strength of evidence rather than the power of an assertion. Habitually powerful members of a group may have to learn to say less; the shy and reticent child must feel encouraged to express a point of view.

Listening to others' viewpoints – are children prepared to take seriously ideas which differ from their own?

Listening to another point of view is just as important as expressing one. Younger children in particular may be more egocentric and find this difficult. Discourse in science should take the form of rational debate. The development of the skill of listening to the views of others is not only important to science; it will have implications right across the curriculum, and beyond. A classroom in which a climate of respect for others' ideas has been achieved enables supportive and constructive debate to take place.

While the development of these social skills will lead to more effective group work in science, it is also true to say that, from the perspective of the development of social skills, practical science activities actually offer opportunities for developing life-skills.

Appendix Ia

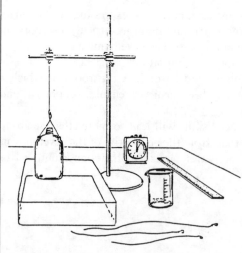

<u>WATER SPRINKLER</u>

STAR Practical Assessment

Apparatus

Retort stand (approx. 1 metre
    high)
Clamp, dowel and clothes peg
Water tray
Plastic sheet
Graduated beaker, 250 ml
Large water container, e.g. plastic
    bucket
1 metre rule
Stop clock/stop watch
Plastic flask with wire hanger,
    and holes in base. Second flask
    having smaller holes
Selection of threads. Tape
    recorder and tapes
Pupil response sheet and pencil

<u>SETTING UP THE CLASSROOM EXPERIENCE</u>   <u>Check-list
                                                items</u>

The seed-tray sprinkler activity should be set up
a few days before the practical assessment, but
not more than two weeks in advance. Aim for
about one week's exposure.

DISCUSSION OF THE CLASSROOM ACTIVITIES   Critical
Reflection

Start the tape recorder. Establish whether the   CR.1 ①
child actively participated in the classroom   CR.2 ②
experience/deliberately watched while others   CR.3 ③
were engaged. (Have a copy of the poster   CR.4 ④
available.) Open discussion of the various ways   CR.5 ⑤
in which the problem was tackled, by the child
and by other children in the class. Ask whether
what was done solved the problem. Ask for any
suggestions for improvement.

INTRODUCTION OF EQUIPMENT

'You've seen some of these things before; some
things are new; let's have a look at all of them
because you might want to use them . . . etc.'

Briefly demonstrate the use of the stop-clock/
stop-watch. Establish use of stop-clock, ruler
and measuring jug, for measuring time, length
and volume.
(Do not attempt to draw attention to units of
measurement.)

'I've also got paper and pencil for you to use
later, if you want to.'

COMPARISON OF BOTTLES (OBSERVATION)   Observing

Put the pink bottles in front of the child   0.5 ⑥
'Tell me what you notice about these'   0.4 ⑦
Prompt 'Anything else?'
If necessary 'What is different about them?'
'In what ways are they the same?'
Remove the non-task bottle

SETTING UP THE SPRINKLER

Assemble the apparatus

Wind a thread onto the dowel and fasten it
with a peg so that the hook hangs about 25 cm
above the base of the container. (Ensure that
the base of the bottle will not foul the base or
walls of the container.) Draw the thread taut
between finger and thumb to remove any twist.

Pick up the pink bottle and explain that you
will cover the holes while the child pours some
water into the bottle, and then the bottle will
be suspended from the hook, and released.
(Avoid request for hypothesis at this point.)
Allow the child to almost fill the bottle, but not
overfill.

FIRST OBSERVATION OF SPRINKLER   Observing

'Thank you. That's enough.   0.1 (8)
Watch carefully and tell me what you notice, 0.2 (9)
when I let go. Make sure you mention
everything you notice.'

Release the bottle.

Let the bottle spin until it reverses and begins
to speed up; then stop it. Ask for further
observations. Prompt 'What else did you notice?'

Remove the bottle and run finger and thumb
down the thread to stop any movement.

SECOND OBSERVATION OF SPRINKLER   Observing

'Let's look at it again.'   0.1 (8)
Repeat the procedure. Invite further   0.2 (9)
observations.

Allow just enough time for the change of
direction to be commented on i.e. one turn in
reverse direction.
If the change was not noted say
'Did you see how the bottle changed direction?'
(Indicate with a circular hand movement)
If the child shows any doubt, repeat. Otherwise
proceed.

PROPOSAL OF INVESTIGATION   Recording

Ask, 'I wonder whether the bottle spins   R.1 ⑩
as much after it's emptied as it did   R.2 ⑪
when the water was coming out?'
(Accompany the question with hand
movements indicating the two directions
in which the bottle turned)

'I'd like you to do an investigation to   Measuring
find out. You can use any of this
equipment. You can change things. You
can do it more than once, if you want.'

Present the recording sheet with the
question at the top of the page. Tell the
child that (s)he can use any of the
apparatus to find the answer to the
question. Tell the child that the sheet is
'to make notes as you go along if you
want to and to write down what you
find'.

	L E N G T H	V O L U M E	C O U N T S
M.1	⑫	⑰	㉒	㉗
M.2	⑬	⑱	㉓	
M.3	⑭	⑲	㉔	
M.4	⑮	⑳	㉕	
M.5	⑯	㉑	㉖	㉘

Whilst the investigation proceeds, note   Planning
the extent of use of the sheet.

Make tentative judgements about
measuring.

P.1 ㉙
P.5 ㉚
CR.5 ㉛

'Tell me what you found.'   Interpreting
Use response to judge interpreting

I.1 ㉜
I.2 ㉝

ASKING FOR EXPLANATIONS   Hypothesising

'Tell me what you think might be the   H.1 ㉞
reason for the bottle turning when the   H.2 ㉟
water comes out?'   H.3 ㊱
    H.4 ㊲

'Why do you think it turns back in the other direction?'	H.1 ㊳ H.2 ㊴ H.3 ㊵ H.4 ㊶
After accepting answers. 'Can you think of any other possible reasons?'	H.5 ㊷
<u>INTRODUCTION OF OTHER CHILDREN'S DATA</u>	Interpreting
Present the prepared card representing some other pupils' investigation of the effect of length of string. 'Some other children tried changing the length of the string and this is what they found.'	I.1 ㊸ I.2 ㊹ I.4 ㊺
'What do you notice about the length of the string and the amount the bottle turns?'	
'How many seconds do you think the bottle would have turned with the string 40 cm long? How did you decide?'	I.5 ㊻
'If you wanted to find out whether the amount the bottle turns would change if you had a different length of <u>your</u> string, what would you do? We haven't got time for you to do it now, but you can describe to me and show me with these things here what you would do.'	Planning P.1 ㊼ P.2 ㊽ P.3 ㊾ P.4 ㊿ P.5 (51)
Prompt with questions to clarify details, e.g. 'which string?' 'how much water?' 'which bottle?'	
'Now, let's go over that again.' (Ask for a repeat of the whole plan.)	
'Can you think of any way that your plan could be made better? How would you make sure your experiment was fair?'	Critical Reflection CR.1 (52)
'Fine - that would help us find out about whether the length of string makes a difference.'	CR.2 (53) CR.3 (54) CR.4 (55)

RAISING QUESTIONS	Raising Questions	
'What other things could we find out about by doing an investigation with these things?'	RQ.1 RQ.2 RQ.3	⑤⑥ ⑤⑦ ⑤⑧
'Some children wondered whether the kind of string made any difference. What do you think they should do to find out?'	RQ.4	⑤⑨
'Here are some other questions children thought of. Which ones could be answered by doing an investigation?'	RQ.4	⑥⓪

> 1. Does the colour of the bottles make a difference to how they spin?
>
> 2. Why do we have pink bottles?
>
> 3. What would happen if the bottles were round and not flat?

(Show the three questions separately, and briefly probe responses.)

EXAMINATION OF NON-TASK BOTTLE (HYPOTHESES)

'Look at this other bottle.'
(Show the bottle with holes pierced on opposite sides.)

'What do you notice?'

If the information is not volunteered, establish that the holes are smaller, opposite one another, and positioned differently, horizontally and vertically.

	Hypothesising	
'If we put water in the bottle and released it, what would happen?'	H.1 H.2	⑥① ⑥②
'Why do you think that would happen?'	H.3 H.4	⑥③ ⑥④
'Can you think of any other reason?'	H.5	⑥⑤

Appendix Ib

Sprinkler Coding Sheet

Date ________ Observer ______________ Pupil

1

2

COMPARISON OF BOTTLES

Observing

O.5 ⑥
O.4 ⑦

3

INVESTIGATION

Recording

R.1 ⑩
R.2 ⑪

Measuring

	LENGTH	TIMES	VOLUMES	COUNTS
M.1	⑫	⑰	㉒	㉗
M.2	⑬	⑱	㉓	
M.3	⑭	⑲	㉔	
M.4	⑮	⑳	㉕	
M.5	⑯	㉑	㉖	㉘

4

INTRODUCTION OF OTHER CHILDREN'S DATA

Interpreting

I.1 ㊸
I.2 ㊹
I.4 ㊺

I.5 ㊻

Planning

P.1 ㊼
P.2 ㊽
P.3 ㊾
P.4 ㊿
P.5 (51)

5

RAISING QUESTIONS

RQ.1 (56)
RQ.2 (57)
RQ.3 (58)

RQ.5 (59)

RQ.4 (60)

DISCUSSION OF CLASSROOM ACTIVITIES

Critical Reflection

CR.1 ①
CR.2 ②
CR.3 ③
CR.4 ④
CR.5 ⑤

FIRST OBSERVATION OF SPRINKLER

O.1 ⑧
O.2 ⑨

SECOND OBSERVATION OF SPRINKLER

O.1 ⑧
O.2 ⑨

DISCUSSION

Planning

P.1 ㉙
P.5 ㉚
CR.5 ㉛

Interpreting

I.1 ㉜
I.2 ㉝

Hypothesising

H.1 ㉞
H.2 ㉟
H.3 ㊱
H.4 ㊲

H.1 ㊳
H.2 ㊴
H.3 ㊵
H.4 ㊶

H.5 ㊷

Critical Reflection

CR.1 (52)
CR.2 (53)
CR.3 (54)
CR.4 (55)

Examination of Non-Task Bottle

Hypothesising

H.1 (61)
H.2 (62)
H.3 (63)
H.4 (64)
H.5 (65)

Interpolation of Missing Value in Table:

(66) [|]

Appendix Ic

'Does the bottle spin as much after it's emptied as it did when the water was coming out?'

Appendix II
Percentage success at each checkpoint
Year six children, 1988

Check-point number	Boys (n=47)	Girls (n=44)	All (n=91)	Check-point number	Boys (n=47)	Girls (n=44)	All (n=91)
1	71	75	73	34	51	64	57
2	25	32	29	35	79	55	67**
3	21	32	27	36	51	21	36**
4	0	4	2	37	15	2	9*
5	0	7	4	38	55	39	47
6	79	80	79	39	75	61	68
7	96	98	97	40	30	30	30
8	98	100	99	41	0	2	1
9	77	80	78	42	19	16	18
10	15	18	17	43	79	84	81
11	38	36	37	44	62	61	62
12	9	7	8	45	19	25	22
13	4	2	3	46	38	50	44
14	2	0	1	47	89	89	89
15	2	0	1	48	75	80	77
16	2	0	1	49	57	61	59
17	49	57	53	50	30	36	33
18	43	52	47	51	70	75	73
19	38	52	45	52	32	36	34
20	32	34	33	53	6	11	9
21	6	14	10	54	21	25	23
22	10	23	17	55	2	0	1
23	19	27	23	56	49	52	51
24	17	23	20	57	57	50	54
25	4	9	7	58	11	16	13
26	0	0	0	59	36	36	36
27	11	9	10	60	57	77	67*
28	4	0	2	61	79	91	85
29	66	86	76*	62	45	50	47
30	53	59	56	63	43	43	43
31	17	39	28*	64	26	11	19
32	62	59	60	65	15	25	20
33	30	25	28				

* = Significant difference P<0.05; ** = P<0.01.

Appendix III
Sequenced checklist of AT1 criteria for KS1 and KS2

┌─ OBSERVING ───

1a observe familiar materials and events in their immediate
    environment, at first hand, using their senses.   ☐

2b identify simple differences, such as *hot/cold, rough/smooth*.   ☐

3b identify and describe simple variables that change over time, *such
    as growth of a plant.*   ☐

3d select and use simple instruments to enhance observations, for
    example, *a stop clock or hand lens.*   ☐

4e select and use a range of measuring instruments, as appropriate, to
    quantify observations of physical quantities, such as volume and
    temperature.   ☐

└──

┌─ RAISING QUESTIONS ─────────────────────────────────

2a ask questions and suggest ideas of the 'how', 'why' and 'what will
    happen if' variety.   ☐

4a raise questions in a form which can be investigated.   ☐

5a use concepts, knowledge and skills to suggest simple questions and
    design investigations to answer them.   ☐

└──

---- HYPOTHESISING ----

3a formulate hypotheses ('*this ball will bounce higher . . .*').

- -

4b formulate testable hypotheses.

---- FOLLOWING INSTRUCTIONS ----

4f follow written instructions and diagrammatic representations.

---- PLANNING ----

3c distinguish between a 'fair' and an 'unfair' test.

- -

4c construct 'fair tests'.

- -

4d plan an investigation where the plan indicated that the relevant variables have been identified and others controlled.

- -

5b identify and manipulate relevant independent and dependent variables, choosing appropriately between ranges, numbers and values.

---- SAFETY ----

4g carry out an investigation with due regard to safety.

---- MEASURING ----

2c use non-standard and standard measures (*hand spans; rulers*).

- -

3e quantify variables, as appropriate, to the nearest labelled division of simple measuring instruments, e.g. *a rule*.

- -

5c select and use measuring instruments to quantify variables and use more complex measuring instruments with the required degree of accuracy, e.g. *minor divisions on thermometers and forcemeters*.

┌─── RECORDING ──────────────────────────────────────┐

2d list and collate observations.   □

- -

2f record findings in charts, drawings, other appropriate forms.   □

- -

3f record experimental findings, e.g., *in tables and bar charts*.   □

- -

3g interpret simple pictograms   □

- -

4h record results by appropriate means, such as the construction of   □
    simple tables, bar charts, line graphs.

└───┘

┌─── INTERPRETING ───────────────────────────────────┐

2e interpret findings by associating one factor with another (*pupils'*   □
    perceptions – 'light objects float', 'thin wood is bendy').

- -

3h interpret observations in terms of a generalised statement, e.g., *the*   □
    greater the suspended weight, the longer the spring.

- -

4i draw conclusions from experimental results.   □

└───┘

┌─── COMMUNICATING ──────────────────────────────────┐

1b describe and communicate their observations, ideally through   □
    talking in groups or by other means, within their class.

- -

3i describe activities carried out by sequencing the major features.   □

- -

4j describe investigations in the form of ordered prose, using a   □
    limited technical vocabulary.

- -

5d make written statements of the patterns derived from the data   □
    obtained from various sources.

└───┘

References

Cavendish S., Galton M., Hargreaves L. and Harlen W. (1990) *Assessing Science in the Primary Classroom: Observing Activities*, Paul Chapman Publishing, London.

DES (1985) *Science 5–16: A Statement of Policy*, HMSO, London.

DES (1988) *Task Group on Assessment and Testing*, DES, London.

Brown C. and Young B. (1982) *Exploring Primary Science*, Cambridge University Press, Cambridge.

Ennever L. (1972) *Science 5/13*, Simon and Schuster, London.

Gilbert C. and Matthews P. (1981) *LOOK!*, Oliver and Boyd, Edinburgh.

Harlen W. (1985) *Primary Science . . . Taking the Plunge*, Heinemann, London.

Harlen W., Darwin A. and Murphy M. (1977) *Match and Mismatch: Raising Questions*, Oliver and Boyd, Edinburgh.

Harlen W., Black P. and Johnson S. (1981) *Science in Schools, Age 11: Report No 1*, HMSO, London.

Harlen W., Black P., Johnson S. and Palacio D. (1983) *Science in Schools, Age 11: Report No 2*, DES, London.

Harlen W., Black P., Johnson S., Palacio D. and Russell T. (1984) *Science in Schools, Age 11: Report No 3*, DES, London.

Harlen W., Palacio D. and Russell T. (1984) *APU Science Report for Teachers, 4, Science Assessment Framework, Age 11*, DES, London.

Harlen W., Black P., Khaligh N., Palacio D. and Russell T. (1985) (ed.) *Science in Schools Age 11: Report No. 4*, DES, London.

Jelly S. (1985) Helping Children Raise Questions and Answering Them, in Harlen W. (ed.) *Primary Science . . . Taking the Plunge*, Heinemann, London.

Kruger C. and Summers M. (1988) *Primary School Teachers' Understanding of Science Concepts – General Overview, Working Paper No 1*, PSTS Project, Oxford University Department of Educational Studies.

Luria A. R. (1976) *Cognitive Development, its Cultural and Social Foundations*, Harvard University Press, Harvard.

NCC (1989) Science Non-Statutory Guidance, National Curriculum Council.

Richards R., Collis M. and Kincaid D. (1985) *Learning Through Science*, Simon and Schuster, London.

Russell T. (ed.), Black P., Harlen W., Johnson S. and Palacio D. (1988) *Science at Age 11, A Review of APU Survey Findings 1980–84*, HMSO, London.

Russell T., Harlen W. and Watt D. (1989) Children's Ideas About Evaporation, *International J. Sci. Ed.*, Vol.II, Special Issue, 566–76.

Schilling M., Harlen W., Hargreaves L. and Russell T. (1990) *Assessing Science in the Primary Classroom: Written Tasks*, Paul Chapman Publishing, London.

Index